INTO ACTION

ALCOHOLICS FOR JESUS

DOUG McPHILLIPS

Also, by Doug McPhillips:

Other Visionary Stories:

NOVELS.
From Darkness to Light.
Awake to my Gutted Dream.
The Sword of Discernment.
Santiago Traveller.
I Prophet.
Master's at my table.
The Guru of Jerusalem.
We are upside down. (Biography)
The Wicklow Way.
The Adventures of Ace McDice.
Instant Karma & Grace.
The Credo.
Reflections of an Old Man.
Reincarnation of the Assassin
Masters of Introspection.
Journey to a hermit's haven.
The Rise and Rise of a 4th Reich
Grandad's tales are tall and true.
A Camino Guide Book.

Country Camino. (Album).
Santiago Traveller. (Album).
Soul Fact. (Album).

Apart from any fair dealing for private study, research, criticism or review, as permitted under the Copyright Act, no part may be reproduced by any process without the editor's written permission.

Doug McPhillips Circa 2025

ISBN. 978-1-763886810

National Library of Australia Catalogue-in-Publication data: New Holy Bible, International Version, Hodder & Stoughton, 1980. Alcoholics Anonymous, 4th Edition, AA World Service, 1976.
As Bill sees it, 8th Print, AA World Service. 2017
Daily Reflections, 11th Print, AA World Service 2014.
Journey to the Inner Mountain, Hodder & Staughton, James Cowan, 2002.
The Choice is always ours, Jove Publishing, 1997.
Santiago traveller, Ingram Spark, Doug McPhillips, 2018.
Google research- Authors Unknown.

This book blends fact and fiction. All characters in this novel are either factual or fictional, and the names of people living at the time may be real or imagined. Any resemblance to actual events, locales, or persons, living or dead, is purely coincidental; however, what is applicable is indeed real. Where poetic license transforms fact into fiction, names have been altered to protect the innocent.

Preface

This book serves as guidance for alcoholics seeking a route to recovery through the Steps of Alcoholics Anonymous, including the concepts of a Higher Power and the spiritual healing that may follow.

Whilst the book offers acceptance to those of faith in any mode of belief, or no belief at all, its primary focus is on a Christian belief in Jesus as a higher power for the recovering alcoholic, in contrast to other forms of belief.

The author makes no apology for his dogma of faith, which is based on the Big Book of Alcoholics Anonymous, Catholic theology, and Biblical guidance from both the Old and New Testaments, primarily from the King James Bible. These form the core of his beliefs, which he now offers to revise in this context.

The book can therefore be regarded as a resource for those who believe in a Higher Power to strengthen their faith, for agnostics and atheists open to considering alternative views on staying sober day by day, and for still-suffering alcoholics seeking spiritual freedom from their disease.

"Alcoholics often gain insight into the instinctual nature of their behaviours, which is primarily driven by destructive drinking. We were drinking to drown our fears, frustrations, and depression. We drank to escape guilt and passion, drinking again to cultivate even more love. We drank in vain glory or foolishly inflated dreams, along with feelings of grandeur, pomp, and power. The state of my alcoholism allowed me to bury my regrets and ' sins of omission, Resentments were buried deep, and I needed to free myself from those, too. I needed to confront my anger and thoughts of revenge."[Extract from page 41 of this book.]

Letter of Introduction

As a sober alcoholic, I have come to believe in the power of God, through Jesus Christ, in all things in my life. It was not always this way; I became dependent on alcohol to cope with life's ups and downs. I drank heavily for more than four decades. However, tragic circumstances and the collapse of my material world forced me to change my direction in life and embrace a spiritual path, living in this world but not being of the world, so to speak.

When I reached the depths of despair and hopelessness, I initially turned to drinking as a crutch to get through each day. As fate would have it, I ended up in a rehabilitation unit to dry out, recover from depression, and learn through guidance how to live again. Then, by a miracle—or so it now seems—I was led to the rooms of Alcoholics Anonymous. With the friendships and guidance of fellow alcoholics and the twelve-step programme, I have remained sober one day at a time for nearly a decade now, although I've been involved in the programme since 2008. When I first joined AA, we shared our stories for the benefit of our fellow alcoholics. We worked on a structure detailing what happened when we drank, what changed, and what life is like now. I will keep it brief here, except to say that when everything went pear-shaped, alcohol became my best mate, and when I reached complete despair, I had no choice but to give it up. With the support of sponsorship and the kindness of fellow alcoholics—who are now my long-term friends—I learned to stay sober one day at a time. More importantly, I learned to embrace the AA steps outlined in the Big Book, a kind of bible for still-suffering alcoholics and those who follow the programme's guiding principles in their day-to-day sobriety.

In my early sobriety, I could only progress through the first three steps. The realisation that I was powerless over alcohol (Step 1) and that I was powerless over everything—including people, places, and things—was earth-shattering to my former egotistical nature and way of life. Then came the understanding that something greater than myself governed the universe; it certainly wasn't Doug and his logical, linear, half-brained view of life. There, I came to believe (Step 2). I woke up, as it were, to a power greater than myself. The scaffolding of my former Christian belief still gripped my heart, but I was in the midst of change. I could no longer find answers to what I had been conditioned to believe all my life. Now, here was a program teaching me to change and accept life on its terms, emphasising what proved to be the most challenging step: surrendering to a God of my understanding (Step 3) as a guiding influence in my life.

For the next decade, I embraced a traditional belief in Jesus Christ as the God of my understanding, as articulated in the AA Steps program. My belief was accompanied by an in-depth search for evidence regarding the reality of Christ's time on earth, including proof of his birth, death, resurrection, and the miracles attributed to him. I had no reservations about referencing the Old Testament prophecies concerning a saviour and the recorded history of Jesus' life in the New Testament. However, these were the only sources confirming Christ's existence during the Roman Empire.

I explored the writings of Cicero on religious belief and those of the Greek philosopher Xenophanes on faith in a single God versus faith in many gods. Various gods depended on one's thoughts and feelings at any given moment, tapping into ethereal spirits that eased the senses. I investigated Egyptian culture, Aboriginal beliefs, and a spectrum of religious traditions, including Buddhism, Roman practices, Judaism, and Christianity. However, I first compared Christ's birth, death, and resurrection with the ancient Mayans' recordings and interpretations of the stars, sun, moon, and planets. The ancient Maya worshipped the Sun God and reportedly documented the Sun's journey from rise to set into darkness during an eclipse, only to rise again after three days, similar to the

Christian belief in Christ's death and resurrection. Thus, I was led to research avatars that predated Christ, such as Buddha, Krishna, Odysseus, Romulus, Dionysus, Heracles, Glycon, the son of Apollo, Zoroaster, Artis of Phrygia, and Horus. While the merits of such beliefs may have drawn many parallels, it was Jesus for whom my search was most extensive, as that was the belief I had been indoctrinated with as a child.

I explored Jesus as the centre of Christian doctrine in the earliest Jesus movement. People spoke of the living Jesus, who preached and was crucified on the cross by the Romans at the request of contemporary Jewish leaders. Preachers and Jesus' apostles proclaimed the spirit of Jesus, making him present in their witness. The New Testament writers—Matthew, Mark, Luke, and John—documented historical accounts discussing the spirit of Jesus. Such was the charisma of the early Christian church that it eventually called for some form of regulation.

I examined the writings of historical scribes whose references to Jesus affirmed that the living Christ indeed walked the earth. The works of Josephus (AD 37-100), a 1st-century Roman-Jewish historian, Tacitus, a Roman historian of the same period, and Secundus (16-112 AD), a lawyer, author, and magistrate known as Pliny the Younger, among others, documented the living Jesus, his death, and his reported resurrection from the dead. Additionally, Marben Separion, Lucian, and Samosata, to name a few, recorded historical evidence of Jesus's existence that aligns with the biblical record. Thus, both biblical and non-biblical historical evidence supported and reinforced my belief that a living Christ sacrificed and died for humanity. We are born so that we may live in the spirit, by the forgiveness of sins that Christians profess, which is our hope and salvation if we embrace him, as his spirit lives within us.

The evidence I uncovered proved beyond a reasonable doubt that Jesus existed. Despite any myths to the contrary, my belief in Him provides a solid foundation for practising the steps of AA, particularly the third step of surrendering to God's guidance through Jesus Christ in my daily life. For the next decade, I remained sober one day at a time, following the steps of AA with a logical, linear approach to my actions, firmly believing in Jesus as my Higher Power. This approach worked well, as I attended three meetings weekly, read the Big Book, and engaged in prayer, meditation, and reflection, as AA had taught me.

Feeling content with my recovery and believing I had experienced a spiritual awakening, I embarked on my third Camino de Santiago pilgrimage to reconcile my most profound spiritual pursuits with my everyday life. After completing the Camino, I travelled to Ireland, the land of my ancestors, to undertake further pilgrimages. I had been away from home and the AA program for about six weeks. I never thought of God, prayer, or meditation during my absence. Consequently, I drank again, which meant I had to restart the program upon my return to Australia. I abandoned my previous logical and linear perspective of Christ as my Higher Power. Since Christ reportedly rose from the dead, I began to use my creative imagination to visualise Jesus as a manifested Risen Saviour. This approach proved effective for several years until I finally addressed Steps 4 through 12. I discovered that I needed to integrate both my logical and creative methods to embrace the reality of Christ, believing in both rational and imaginative ways to put the AA programme into practice. What has emerged is an exploration of my findings, drawing parallels between the 12-step programme and the New Testament, creating a living template for believers in Jesus as he relates to fellow alcoholics and those of us still searching for conviction. Additionally, the Old Testament records the history of the Jewish faith and the coming of the Saviour, while tracing Jesus' lineage. It may interest those who wish to delve deeper into profound beliefs, but it is a subplot to the novel's essence.

CHAPTER I.

POWERLESS

Interestingly, feeling powerless is equivalent to being helpless. This mindset provides a solid foundation for embarking on a spiritual journey. Why is that? The more a person becomes aware of their powerlessness and the more desperate they feel, the more likely they are to seek help.

The Bible discusses powerlessness extensively but emphasises the spiritual aspect more than the physical—poor in spirit, poverty of spirit, spiritual poverty, spiritual weakness, etc. It may be that humanity, as a living being, derives existence and power from the Spirit of God (Job 32:8; 33:4).

Recognising and acknowledging failure, along with our sense of powerlessness, exposes our complete dependence on something or someone beyond ourselves. Given our flawed nature and awareness of the death of body, mind, and spirit, this feeling of powerlessness is essential for conversion.

Without a sense of overriding dependence, we will never turn to God in the first place. Lacking this sense of need, we will not continually seek Him, as our passivity would indicate that, much like the Christian community in the ancient Roman city of Laodicea, we believe we need nothing and are sufficient unto ourselves. Even when we profess to believe, we can become overconfident, as Peter did, who boasted that, unlike others, he would never desert Christ, only to fall flat on his face in spiritual failure. The sense of growth in Christian character primarily lies in realising our powerlessness and acknowledging it before God.

The Avatars who came before Christ and those who followed seemed to have unique qualities or gifts; yet, they also endured great suffering and faced serious challenges. A key idea in the writings of the Baha'i Faith is that these remarkable figures, called "Manifestations of God," appear human in history but also seem "almost God-like," much like how we likely seem to a house dog that has no understanding of our university education.

Our primary focus here is Jesus and his connection to the foundation of AA, established by its founders, Bill Wilson and Dr. Bob Smith. This includes the concept of a Higher Power, which requires faith and trust to recover from alcoholism through the 12-step programme.

It was through experiencing a state of hopelessness, despair, and misery that I, like those founders, discovered my profound powerlessness over alcohol, people, places, and things. I lost my faith in the indoctrinated Christian teachings of my childhood, as I found no answers to my dilemma there. For a time, I adopted an atheistic attitude, and my uncertainty persisted, so to speak; for quite a while, I identified as agnostic. This was not for lack of trying, as I delved into various doctrines to recover from the well of despair I encountered. Eventually, I had to surrender to God in my powerlessness.

Interestingly, Jesus demonstrated great power and authority in the Bible. However, there are times when he seemed powerless, such as during his crucifixion or when he faced mockery and insults. His community in Nazareth disowned him, and many of those claiming to be his followers turned away. They focused on his human weakness rather than his spiritual strength.

A prime example of Jesus' powerlessness is found in the Garden of Gethsemane, where he reportedly wept tears of blood, aware that he was to suffer death on the Cross. It may be interpreted that he perceived the flaws of humanity throughout history. Despite the impending sacrifice he was about to make to redeem humanity from sin, people would continue to follow the world's ways instead of the spiritual path we are meant to tread. The lessons from Christ's experience in the Garden emphasise the importance of prayer, sacrifice, the redeeming value of suffering, and love for our fellow man.

Bill Wilson, the co-founder of Alcoholics Anonymous, had, like me, been raised in Christianity as a child. Similarly, in his adult life, he abandoned the faith and, during his darkest hours of despair and hopelessness as an alcoholic, experienced a period of atheistic thought before embracing the six steps of the Oxford Group and finding belief in a Higher Power. I have little doubt that Bill viewed Jesus as his faithful God. In a conversation with another alcoholic at a sobriety meeting held in a church, he was asked, "Where is God?" Bill pointed to a painting of Jesus in the Garden of Gethsemane and replied, "He is there."

It may surprise many present-day AA members who are ardent followers of the Big Book that, in its first version, particularly in the chapter titled "There is a Solution," there was a firm insistence that the solution to alcoholism is fundamentally "religious" in nature—a term that brings considerable weight to the discussion. Perhaps none would be more surprising than Dr. Jung's assertion that the only hope for recovery from drinking is found in a "vital religious experience"—a notably different prescription from the often-cited "vital spiritual experience" found in the Big Book today.

As Bill was writing the first version of this chapter, he recognised the problem. He continually reminded the reader that when he uses the term "religious," he intends it to be understood in the most flexible and open-ended way possible. He urges the reader to maintain an open mind regarding the question of religion, claiming that the term is meant to encompass "nearly every conceivable shade of belief" and stating that "we have no desire to convince anyone that the true God can only be discovered in some particular way." The religious solution is explicitly understood to be as accommodating as possible, allowing individuals to approach and resolve any issues they might have with God in whatever way they find acceptable. Bill's final appeal to William James's book, The Varieties of Religious Experience, aims to emphasise that he is discussing a religious solution that comes without formal dogma and prescribed religious practices.

Later edits to this chapter would significantly reduce the impact and implied message of the word "religious" by repeatedly replacing it with the much gentler "spiritual." That word undoubtedly carries some baggage, but nowhere near as much as the more specific "religious." To most ears, that word almost necessarily implies "church" and "dogma." At the same time, "spiritual" might be understood to relate to a meaningful life independent of any formal religious organisation.

But how open was Bill in this early version of "There Is A Solution" to "nearly every conceivable ... shade of belief"? It does not require a careful reading of the text to realise that Wilson is a man of his time, culture, and upbringing. When he uses the word "religious"—despite all of his protests to the contrary—he identifies with a specific concept of God, to the exclusion of all others. Whatever later liberalisations may have been introduced by the substitution of spiritual for religious or by Bill's consistent efforts over the years to open the doors of A.A. ever more expansively, the open concept claimed for religion here does not embrace a whole host of the "varieties" so candidly acknowledged in William James's book. This study includes investigations into the religious beliefs of Pagans, Hindus, Buddhists, and Sufis (among others). James's Varieties of Religious Experience is a 400-page work of complexity in religious philosophy that James wrote over the years. Its complexity was beautifully broken down by Bill Wilson, who was on a mission to become spiritual when he discovered the work. Bill states that when one embarks upon their spiritual path, they first experience calamity from which there is no turning back. Next follows a mental and/or spiritual collapse in which there seems to be no way out, and finally, there is a cry for help from a Higher power, usually via prayer.

As his language consistently shows, when Wilson uses the word "religious" here, he refers to the belief in a personal, providential God, closely aligned with the God of Abraham, who is the ultimate source of salvation for alcoholics. When it comes to recovery, he is not referring, for instance, to the indifferent Creator God of the Deists or to any of the other more liberal concepts of "God as you understand Him." Bill Wilson's God is "the Creator of you and me," the "living Creator," and "the living God." He is a God with "a loving and powerful hand," capable of "entering into our hearts and lives" where He can "accomplish those things which by no stretch of the imagination were humanly possible." He is a God who wholeheartedly offers each of us the opportunity to form a very personal and direct relationship with Him, and on whom we can rely to help overcome the insanity that precedes the first drink.

He had a great fear that the message might be misunderstood by alcoholics in distant places. It was one thing to pass on the message face-to-face when one could observe the other's reactions and respond to objections, questions, or confusion. In print, there was no second chance…

Like almost everything else in the chapter, this conception of God originated from Bill Wilson's experience. It serves as the foundation of a belief system he adopted when he first got sober and maintained for the rest of his life. Since Bill's understanding of God was providential, one could pray with the full expectation of receiving answers to those prayers—that is, the God he explicitly described as the "glorious" solution to the problem of uncontrolled drinking in this first version of "There Is A Solution."

Deep down in every man, woman, and child lies the fundamental idea of God. It may be obscured by calamity, pomp, or the worship of other things, but it is present in some form or another. Faith in a Power greater than ourselves and the miraculous demonstrations of that Power in human lives are truths as old as man himself. (As Bill Sees It, Page 152.)

Faith may often be given through inspired teaching or convincing personal examples of its fruits. It may sometimes be that he had a reason. For instance, some clergy members believe St. Thomas

Aquinas proves God's existence by sheer logic. But what can one do when all these channels fail? As such, my grievous dilemma.

In the Alcoholics Anonymous Big Book, Bill states, "It was when I came to believe I was powerless over alcohol, only when I appealed to God, who just might exist, that I experienced a spiritual awakening. This freedom-giving experience came first, and faith followed—a gift indeed." Thus, the man who simplistically summarises the essence of William James's complex thesis on spirituality determined that calamity, collapse, and a cry for help from a higher power fostered progress in belief in God.

My path to recovery and spiritual discovery of God was a slow process that, like all forms of enlightenment, did not come quickly. Looking back on it now, it truly was a gradual journey. I lost my family, business, home, community, and most of my friends. For a time, due to my excessive drinking, I lost my enthusiasm for life and my sanity. Like many alcoholics, I attempted a geographical escape into isolation to overcome my blues and quit drinking cold turkey. I lasted six months without a drink, but I was not cured of my alcoholism. Subsequently, I enrolled in a rehabilitation hospital to rest and recuperate from depression and anxiety, as I did not recognise at that point that I was an alcoholic.

It has been said that God works in strange ways. This is certainly true for me, as those I met during my recovery in the hospital had a profound effect on my understanding of my alcoholism, my need to embrace a belief in a Higher Power, and ultimately, a newfound direction in life that I never would have thought possible during those darkest hours of recovery. In my childhood, the religious experience was an indoctrination into the bond with God as a trinity:

Father, Son, and Holy Spirit. This connection was deeper than when I reconnected with what I had been given at birth—a gift from God. Belief in God is the essence of what religiosity means for humanity, but like many who are caught up in the world, I disregarded what was, by nature, my birthright. I was in a predicament, like a coiled spring; I was tightly wound due to the events and tragic circumstances of my life. I was lost and didn't know myself at all. Fear overcame me in a moment of clarity, as I stood on the precipice of what I perceived to be the dragon's mouth of hell on earth. Seated on the floor near my hospital bed, I began to cry. A nurse entered and inquired about what troubled me. I shared my fear, and she said: "Remember the story of the mustard seed in the bible."

The mustard seed parable is key to understanding the vital and influential role our faith in Jesus can play. It reminds us that we have Jesus's power within us when we trust in his strength and might. Jesus used the mustard seed as an analogy to show that even the tiniest amount of faith has great potential. He emphasised that faith can grow and lead to remarkable results, no matter how small it may seem. The faith of a mustard seed is mighty. I used that analogy when I lacked the courage to embrace health during my early recovery. I discovered that a golden thread of consciousness ran through the core of my being. By releasing the coiled spring inside me, I visualised this golden thread as connecting me to God, linking the heavens to the earth. Somehow, this helped me unwind the tightly coiled spring of anxiety and depression that had overwhelmed me. As a result, direction and courage grew with acceptance and growth. It came from trusting in God's gentle, slow work, especially during moments of spiritual awakening, simply living with whatever arose. A fellow patient in the hospital guided me to the doors of AA, and I attended my first meeting as I had no other direction. The doors opened, and I walked in to find a fellowship of like-minded individuals—fellow alcoholics who, like me, had faced hell and back.

My experiences inside the hospital and in AA meetings shared signs of synchronicity and meaningful coincidences. The spiritual core within me, that golden thread, unwound the tightly wound spring of anxiety and depression. My drinking days were now over, and I no longer had a crutch to lean on, but recovery was slow and sometimes painful. I soon learnt that, at my core, I was a loner and an outsider from the inside out. The realisation dawned that I belonged to the 2-3% of the population who no longer fit into the world's ways. I had always been a square peg trying to fit into a round hole; I had mistakenly believed that the world held the answers to my dilemmas. Over time, I began to understand that I was born an outsider, genetically predisposed—like all alcoholics—to be so. It took time to let it sink into the marrow of my bones—the acceptance that brought peace and hope for the adventures ahead in search of spiritual well-being.

I was still fearful of what lay ahead, and as it happened, I realised that I needed to enter the dragon's mouth of my ultimate fear. No longer having the crutch of alcohol to bury my fear, I had to take a leap of faith to descend into the pit of darkness. The dragon's mouth transformed into a lotus flower of creative ideas. I began writing songs and books, which I continue to do. However, despite being sober, I had not sufficiently let go to free-fall. God had provided a way out, but my songwriting and book writing felt like a residual parachute. My creativity became a cathartic means of expressing my inner feelings, which may benefit others, but at the same time, there remains the risk of egocentric behaviour.

Surrendering the ego and accepting the God of my understanding as the path to spiritual wholeness was a gradual process that took time. In the past, I often veered off track, seeking answers in the arms of another woman, which posed a danger of disrupting the natural order of things. This only ever brought me splinters and setbacks on my spiritual journey. Additionally, there remains a risk of becoming entangled in the world. Ego recognition also appears in my books and songs. Like all life lessons, it's a learning curve. I regained my belief in God by detaching from the world I once knew and embracing a sense of powerlessness. It came to me as an awakening of the spirit through my imagination, rather than through the logical, linear belief I had been indoctrinated with in my later years, when I lived for money, power, and fame. So, I found the middle road, realising it can't be achieved by linear, rational, sequential, or logical means. Those are the half-brained notions of the world at large. The way of the spirit and imagination is the third way, tempered by a boat of personality. It involves floating on the spiritual waters of life, setting the sail and adjusting the rudder of existence from within the spiritual core. All it takes is a gentle touch of the rudder to stay on course.

CHAPTER 2.

CAME TO BELIEVE

We seek the inner truth, which becomes the universal truth. The truth of St. Augustine's confessions resonates: "Faith is to believe what we cannot yet see; the reward of this faith is to know what you think." In another prayer, Augustine states: "You have made us for yourself, O Lord, and our heart is restless until it rests in you."

When I lost my family, business, home, and hope for the future, I also lost my faith in God. No matter how hard I tried to regain my belief and some semblance of power, nothing changed despite my best efforts to pray and request the infinite God of all to restore me to my former glory. Overwhelmed by depression and a sense of hopelessness, I tried to numb my pain through excessive drinking. Several years later, I rediscovered faith in a God of my understanding through the 12-step AA programme.

In the first decade of my newfound faith, I attended three meetings a week, engaged with the Big Book and spiritual readings, and actively practised what I had learnt for the benefit of the still-suffering alcoholic. Traditional, logical, linear thinking, aligned with the steps, seemed to partially address what I had pieced together about Jesus' life. It paralleled what I read in the New Testament and my childhood faith. However, during my last pilgrimages to Spain and Ireland, I had been away from the programme for six weeks, had not read any spiritual books, and did not pray or even think about God. It felt like I was finding my way without needing a spiritual programme. Consequently, I drank again, but my years of Christian indoctrination and the past decade in AA made me realise I couldn't slip back into my old drinking habits. Upon returning home to Australia, I began to rekindle my faith in a Higher Power, focusing more on the Risen Christ through my imaginative reflections.

It was a God of the manifest who seemed to help me remain sober one day at a time for a few years. Then, one day, I realised that the brain consists of two parts: logical, linear reasoning and creative imagination. I believe it might be worth a shot to unite the two. What soon became evident in my daily practice of believing in God while practising and living the AA way of life is the presence of God in the manifest and God in my heart through the 12 Steps, as I perceive Him to be, which is the essence of my faith. So, once I came to believe in a God of my understanding in a more enlightened way, I began to view Christ on earth in a different light—the man on a spiritual mission who ultimately sacrificed himself for the sins of humanity.

The thought of Jesus, at the age of twelve, teaching the priests and rabbis in the temple in Jerusalem about the true meaning of the written word of God must have been astonishing to these scholarly men of biblical doctrine. To see this boy possessing greater insight into the word of God than they had, despite their doctrines of faith, must have been remarkable. Recorded history highlights Jesus, who never wrote a word of his beliefs or teachings, which may seem uneducated to some. However, as a Jewish boy, he would have been taught scripture from an early age, and his mathematical mind must have been sharp as he practised carpentry as a young man with Joseph, his foster father.

Regarding his lineage, Abraham is recognised as the ancestral figure in the Bible and is central to the Jewish, Christian, and Islamic faiths. Jesus is depicted as a descendant of Abraham who fulfilled a promise to Abraham and his descendants. As the Son of Abraham, Jesus represents a new Abraham, the founder of a new chosen people. He will play a role in God's plan similar to that of Abraham. Matthew could have traced Jesus' ancestry back to Adam, as Luke does in his genealogy of Jesus (3:23-38).

So here was Jesus, who, before his last three years, had determined to become a human sacrifice to God for the sins of humanity. Where did he get this idea? His mission was to be a sacrificial lamb. As was the Jewish custom of biblical times and indeed during Jesus's lifetime on earth, the Jewish people would offer their best lamb to be sacrificed on the altar in the temple of Jerusalem. The High Priest would later slaughter the lamb of the offering as a burnt offering, and the people would pray upon the ascending smoke; in turn, they would eat the flesh of the lamb in homage to God.

The biblical story of Abraham's offering of his son Isaac to God as a sacrifice parallels Christ's later self-offering. One day, when Isaac was a boy, God came to Abraham and instructed him to sacrifice Isaac on Mt. Moriah. Although he loved his son dearly, Abraham did not hesitate to obey the Lord. The next day, he saddled his donkey and began the journey with Isaac, two servants, and wood for the sacrifice. As they approached the mountain, Abraham told the servants to stay behind while he and Isaac ascended. They reached the location God had specified and built an altar. Abraham bound Isaac, arranged the wood on the altar, and drew his knife.

But at that moment, an angel stopped him. Genesis 22:11-12 describes:

But the angel of the Lord called to him from heaven, "Abraham, Abraham!" "Here I am," he answered. "Do not lay a hand on the boy," said the angel. "Do not do anything to him. For now, I know that you fear God since you did not withhold from me your son, your only son."

Perhaps Jesus, knowing the story of his ancestor Abraham and his offering of his son Isaac from Holy Scripture, had determined to offer himself to God as a human sacrifice since his youth. Having witnessed many offerings from the people, whether a lamb as a sacrifice to God or the account of Abraham offering Isaac, his son, as a human sacrifice, he resolved to be a sacrificial lamb and embarked on his mission to fulfil that purpose.

On his days off working as a carpenter, we can picture the young man from Nazareth on a four-day hike along the rugged mountain trail to the Sea of Galilee. Doubtless, he found places to rest during the evenings and reached the sea early in the day aboard a fishing vessel heading for the beach along the Galilean coastline, where fishing vessels unloaded their catch to be sold at nearby markets.

We may visualise the young Yeshua Ben Yosef, known as Jesus before Christianity, coining the name Jesus and fluent in Hebrew, Aramaic, and Greek, conversing with fishermen in their native tongue. Mostly, they were Galileans of Jewish descent, but no doubt other nationalities also came to the Sea of Galilee to make a living fishing. He must have already had his mission to preach to the people about the Kingdom of God, guiding them on the spiritual path to salvation and ultimately toward his impending sacrifice, as he did at the Last Supper. Meanwhile, he would have carefully assessed the character and personality of his chosen twelve Apostles. He would have observed Simon, the captain of his fishing vessel, giving orders to his crew, marking him as the one who would be called Peter, upon whose foundation he would become the leader of the fledgling community after his death on the Cross.

While His chosen apostles learned from Jesus about the kingdom of heaven and His interpretation of the Torah, Jesus, in turn, learned much from them about the kingdom of men, human nature, and their world at the time. These twelve men represented various types of human temperament and had not been made *alike* by schooling. Many of these Galilean fishermen carried heavy strains of gentile blood due to the forcible conversion of the gentile population of Galilee one hundred years earlier. All of them, except the Alpheus twins and possibly Judas Iscariot, were graduates of the synagogue schools, having been thoroughly trained in the Hebrew scriptures and much of the current knowledge of that day. Seven were graduates of the Capernaum synagogue schools, and there was no better nor worse among those chosen by James and John Zebedee, specifically James and Judas, the sons of Alpheus of Greek origin, as was Judas Iscariot, who had been introduced to Jesus by the gentle Nathanael, one of the chosen few.

Apart from choosing Peter for his leadership qualities, his brother Andrew, who was about a year older than Jesus, was selected for his excellent administrative skills. While he was a fisherman like the others, he was not a preacher. He made a good teacher for those who would spread the message Jesus taught about the kingdom of heaven. Then came James, the elder of the two apostles, son of Zebedee. James and his brother John were known as "Sons of Thunder," as it seems they inherited their father's quick temper, which was James' main fault. Jesus chose him because he was level-headed in his thinking and planning, and was never in a hurry, although he could sometimes be moody and quiet. It appeared that James understood Jesus' message better than the others and was often seen alone with Jesus discussing his mission on earth. It may be that his size and strength were added reasons for his selection during difficult times, serving as a sort of bodyguard. However, this may have been a later interpretation; it probably referred to his courage and spiritual strength when facing beheading at the hands of King Herod. Agrippa

Let's assess each of the apostles based on their merit. John Zebedee, the brother of James, was the youngest of the twelve and worked as a fisherman alongside his brother. Peter, James, and John served as Jesus' three principal aides, staying closer to him than the other apostles. Philip was the fifth apostle chosen after meeting John during his journey with the Lord between the Jordan and Galilee. From readings, it's clear that he was influenced by the acceptance of Jesus as the deliverer by Andrew, Peter, James, and John. Nathaniel, as mentioned earlier, was chosen by Jesus himself. He stood out for being inclined toward philosophy and a bit of a dreamer. He took Jesus' message more seriously than most, yet he didn't take himself too seriously.

James the younger and Judas, the sons of Alpheus, the twin fishermen living near Kheresa, were the ninth and tenth apostles chosen by James, the son of Zebedee. They loved their Master, and Jesus loved them, but they never interrupted his discourses with questions. Although they understood very little about their fellow apostles' philosophical discussions or theological debates, they rejoiced at finding themselves numbered among such a group of mighty men.

The next to join these bands of followers was Matthew. It is recorded that Matthew was a tax collector.. Andrew appointed Matthew as the financial representative of the apostles. He served as the fiscal agent and publicity spokesman for the apostolic organisation. Matthew was a keen judge of human nature and an efficient propagandist. His personality is difficult to visualise, but he was an earnest disciple and an increasingly firm believer in the mission of Jesus and the certainty of the kingdom. Jesus never gave him a nickname, but his fellow apostles commonly referred to him as the "money-getter."

Philip chose Thomas. Later, he was known as "Doubting Thomas" because he initially doubted Jesus' resurrection when told about it by other apostles. Still, his fellow apostles hardly regarded him as a chronic doubter. He famously declared he wouldn't believe unless he could see and touch Jesus's wounds. When Jesus later appeared to him and invited him to do just that, Thomas proclaimed his faith, saying, "My Lord and my God!" This incident is recorded in the Gospel of John. Thomas possessed a logical, sceptical mind and had a form of courageous loyalty that prevented those who knew him well from viewing him as a trifling sceptic. Although he had little formal education, he had a keen, reasoning mind and was the son of excellent parents living in Tiberias. Thomas had the most analytical mind among the twelve; he was the true scientist of the apostolic group.

Simon Peter chose Simon Zelotes as the eleventh apostle. He was a capable man of good lineage who lived with his family in Capernaum. The apostle was a passionate advocate who often spoke impulsively. Before fully committing to the patriotic organisation of the Zealots, he worked as a merchant in Capernaum. Simon was in charge of the leisure and entertainment for the apostolic group, and he was an exceptionally efficient organiser of the twelve's recreational activities.

As mentioned earlier, Judas Iscariot, the twelfth apostle, was chosen by Nathaniel. When he met the apostle in Kerioth, he looked for work with a fish-drying business at the southern end of the Sea of Galilee. He was probably the most educated of the twelve and the only Judean in the Master's apostolic family. Judas didn't have exceptional personal strength, but he showed many outward signs of culture and training. He was a good thinker, but not always a sincere one. Judas didn't fully understand himself; he wasn't honest in his self-assessment. Andrew appointed Judas as treasurer of the twelve, a role for which he was well suited. Until the time of his Master's betrayal, he carried out his duties honestly, faithfully, and efficiently.

Judas admired nothing in Jesus except his generally attractive and exquisitely charming personality. He never managed to rise above his Judean prejudices against his Galilean companions; he even criticised many aspects of Jesus mentally. While eleven apostles saw him as the perfect man, the "one altogether lovely and the chiefest among ten thousand," this self-satisfied Judean often dared to voice criticism in his heart. It can be argued that Judas is unfairly portrayed as a traitor responsible for Jesus' capture and imprisonment. Such a claim could be false, as it suited the early Christians, the New Judaism, who needed a scapegoat to explain why

Jesus was captured. Judas became the most likely person to blame. Some might suggest that Judas, aware of the dangers facing his master during the Jewish Passover, agreed to have Jesus imprisoned for his safety. He was paid thirty pieces of silver for his service, a customary payment in ancient Jewish times.

While there is no concrete proof of what happened during Judas' betrayal, we can speculate that he felt regret and shame. In those moments, he might have timidly imagined, as a mental defence, that Jesus could use his power to save him at the last moment. When he realised he had been deceived by those who insisted on having Jesus crucified, he, overwhelmed with remorse and shame, took his own life. Jesus understood Judas's motives, and though the New Testament describes it as a betrayal, followers of a new-age religion needed someone to blame, and it was Judas. The eleven apostles were horrified and stunned. Jesus looked at the betrayer with only pity. The world has struggled to forgive Judas, and his name has been shunned across a vast universe.

In Step 2 of the AA program, I came to believe in Jesus, the Apostles' message, and the writings of Matthew, Mark, Luke, and John as the account of the life and times of the Lord, along with His fundamental message. In particular, the message of this Step resonated with me: "Come to believe that a Power greater than ourselves could restore us to sanity." It has been statistically proven that alcoholics rarely regain their resources. Even the early pioneers of AA recognised that only the most desperate cases could accept and process this unpalatable truth. Those who came to believe in a God of their understanding and the AA way found healing to lead a seemingly ordinary life.

As it says in Step 2: "When we encountered AA, the fallacy of our defiance was revealed. We had not asked what God's will was for us at that time. Instead, we had been telling Him who He ought to be, interpreting Him misguidedly, distorting who He is and what He wants us to be." Regardless of my view of God, it became clear that belief meant relying on God, not defying Him. Over time in AA, I witnessed the fruits of that reliance—a belief in God that spared fellow members from the final catastrophe. Many calmly accepted impossible situations, neither seeking to run nor to recriminate. Thus, faith has been proven to work under all conditions. This meant that I had to pay whatever price in humility was required.

Having come to terms with this Higher Power, I sought to explore what it meant to be an alcoholic with Jesus as my Higher Power in a spiritual sense. This required me to embrace the next step, surrender to this God of my understanding (Step 3), and allow Him to guide my thoughts, words, and actions. To achieve this, I needed to view Jesus through the lens of the AA programme and the Gospels to gain a more comprehensive perspective on my new philosophy—a spiritual conceptual approach to living in this world but not being of it. An in-depth approach to surrendering was what the apostles practised in their mission for Jesus, both while He was on Earth and after His resurrection and ascension. It seemed that to embody the spirit of Jesus, I needed to understand how to live in the spirit of Jesus. I had been taught about the Father, Son, and Holy Spirit symbolically, along with the Mass, as a reenactment of the Last Supper. However, how can I practice my spiritual beliefs in light of the AA Steps, given my new understanding?

CHAPTER 3.

TURNING OVER TO GOD

Perhaps the most challenging step in staying sober one day at a time is Step 3: "Decided to hand over our will to the care of God as we understand Him." We are expected to surrender entirely to God's will, seeking His guidance and plan for us. Letting go of egocentric behaviour is not easy for anyone, especially for an alcoholic trying to remain sober day by day. In Bill Wilson's story in the Big Book of AA, he had to test his willingness to surrender and make amends for his past behaviours to the best of his ability. As Bill W. states: " I was to test my thinking against the new God-consciousness within. Common sense would thus become uncommon sense. I was to sit quietly when in doubt, asking only for direction and strength to face my problems as He would have me. Never was I to pray for myself, except as my requests related to my usefulness to others. Only then might I expect to receive, for that would be to a great extent." Was Bill talking about God's grace?

On page 85, Chapter 6 of the Big Book 'Into Action," it states: [It is easy to let up on the spiritual program of action and rest on our laurels. We are headed for trouble if we do, for alcohol is a subtle foe. We are not cured of alcoholism. What we have is a daily reprieve contingent on the maintenance of our spiritual condition. Every day, we must carry the vision of God's will into all our activities. "How can I best serve Thee? Thy will, not mine, be done."]

As it says on page 88 of the Big Book [When we take such a humble approach, we are much less in danger of excitement, fear, anger, worry, self-pity or foolish decisions. We become more efficient and do not tire so quickly, for we are not wasting energy foolishly as we did when trying to arrange our lives to suit ourselves. It works; it does.]

In recognising atheists and agnostics, I understand what it means to have an open mind toward a Higher Power without a strict definition. However, this book primarily aims at those who have embraced Jesus as their Higher Power. This may come from previous indoctrination, an enlightening experience like the one Bill W had, or through research like mine, which explores a logical, linear approach to surrendering to a God of my understanding and utilising the creative imagination- engaging the other side of the brain to accept the manifestation of the Risen Christ Jesus.

So, what draws one to a new faith in Jesus as a Higher Power? The recognition of the spirit of the Risen Christ is at the heart of it all. To explore this further, one must turn to the New Testament and, in doing so, like an alcoholic, discuss what occurred, what changed, and what it is like now—initially for the apostles and historically since for those of us who believe in the power of the Holy Spirit through Jesus Christ.

In the second century AD, the Gospel of Matthew was placed at the beginning of the New Testament. It was once thought to be the first Gospel written, although we now recognise that the Gospel of Mark predates it. Since the Gospel is deeply concerned with issues related to Judaism, it serves as an appropriate transition from the Old Testament. Matthew is divided into seven parts. An introductory segment recounts the story of Jesus's miraculous birth and the origin of his ministry. At the same time, a conclusion narrates the Last Supper, Jesus's trial and crucifixion, and the resurrection. In the middle are five structurally parallel sections. Each section features a narrative segment—occasionally interrupted by dialogue and brief homilies—that details Jesus's miracles and actions. Closing each section, Jesus delivers a long sermon that responds to the lessons learned in the narrative. The Sermon on the Mount, which introduces the essential elements of the Christian message, follows Jesus' initial venture into ministry (5: 1–7: 29). The Mission Sermon, which empowers Jesus's apostles, comes after Jesus recognises the need for more teachers and preachers (10: 1–42). The enigmatic Sermon in Parables addresses Jesus' frustration with those who do not understand or accept His message (13:1-52). The Sermon on the Church responds to the need to establish a lasting fellowship of Christians (18 1 35). Finally, the eschatological Sermon, which speaks to the end of the world, addresses the growing certainty that Jesus will be crucified (23:1, 25, 46) within the New Testament of the Christian Bible. Matthew became the most significant of all Gospel texts for first- and second- century Christians because it encompasses all the elements vital to the early church: the story of Jesus' miraculous conception, an explanation of the importance of liturgy, law, discipleship, and teaching, along with an account of Jesus's life and death. The Gospel of Matthew has long been regarded as the most essential of the four.

Although second-century church tradition attributes the Gospel to Matthew, a former tax collector and one of Jesus' Twelve Apostles, also known as Levi, scholars today maintain that there is no direct evidence of Matthew's authorship. Because the Gospel of Matthew relies heavily on the earlier Gospel of Mark and late first-century oral tradition for its description of events in Christ's life, it is unlikely that the author of the Gospel of Matthew was an eyewitness to the life of Christ. Instead, the author was probably a Jewish member of a learned community in which study and teaching were passionate forms of piety, and the Gospel was probably written between 80 and 90 AD.

Matthew traces Jesus' lineage back to Abraham and describes his conception when his mother, Mary, was " found to be with child from the Holy Spirit." Matthew traces his birth, visits from the wise men of the East bearing gifts, visits from humble shepherds, Herod's killing of first-born babies when Jesus was named " King of the Jews, " and the flight into Egypt of the Holy family returning to Nazareth after Herod's death.

Years pass, and Jesus grows up. A man in a loincloth who survives on wild honey and locusts begins to prophesy throughout Judea, announcing Jesus as the one who will come to "baptise you with the Holy Spirit and fire" (3:11). This prophet, John the Baptist- a likely member of the ascetic Jewish community- eventually encounters Jesus. John baptises Jesus, and Jesus receives the blessing of God, who declares, "This is my Son, the Beloved" (3:17). Jesus is led into the wilderness for forty days without food or water to be tested by Satan. Emerging unscathed and triumphant, Jesus preaches his central and most frequently repeated proclamation: "Repent! For the kingdom of heaven has come near" (4:17). His ministry begins.

Matthew mentions the earliest followers of Jesus: Simon, Peter, Andrew, James, and John. He began preaching once Jesus gathered this small group of Jewish believers. His early ministry reaches its peak when he delivers a sermon famously known as the Sermon on the Mount, which profoundly impresses his growing audience (5:1 7:29). The sermon emphasises humility, obedience, love for one's neighbour, the proper way to pray, and trust in God. Jesus states that the poor, meek, and hungry are blessed.

As he travels through Galilee, Jesus continues to attract large crowds. Matthew recounts ten of Jesus's miracles, which are also described in the Gospel of Mark. Jesus heals a leper, a paralytic, a woman with a haemorrhage, a centurion's servant, and Peter's mother-in-law. He also calms a storm, exorcises demons, restores sight to the blind, and raises a girl from the dead. Jesus resolves to "send out labourers" to minister to the Gentiles, whom He calls "lost sheep" (9:38). Jesus appoints twelve disciples, telling them they will face persecution but should not be afraid. He instructs the apostles to proclaim that the "kingdom of heaven has come near" and to heal the sick, raise the dead, cleanse lepers, and cast out demons without charge (10:7).

In Chapter 11, Matthew interrupts his account of Jesus and his disciples' mission to focus on Jesus himself. He recounts the opposition Jesus faces, as some people disapprove of his association with sinners, tax collectors, and prostitutes. They label him a glutton and a drunkard. In the face of such rejection, Jesus does not apologise but admonishes those who reject him.

Jesus responds to his challengers with a series of parables. Matthew describes several parables—the parables of the sower, the weeds, the mustard seed, and the leaven—that Jesus shares with the crowds gathered to listen to him (13:1-33). Jesus then explains that his disciples are part of his family.

Jesus's ministry of healing, cleansing, and raising the dead continues as he travels throughout Galilee. However, he is rejected in his hometown of Nazareth, where his friends and neighbours deride him. He continues to perform miracles, but the people grow increasingly resistant and disbelieving. Jesus multiplies loaves and fish, feeding thousands with very little food. He heals the sick and preaches the message of spiritual righteousness. Yet, Jesus repeatedly finds that his disciples still lack faith in him. When he miraculously walks across the water to them, they assume he must be a ghost. Even after he multiplies the loaves, they fear hunger. Only Simon rightly professes his faith: "You are the Messiah, the Son of the living God" (16:16). Jesus renames Simon "Peter," a name whose Greek form is identical to the Greek word for "rock." Jesus announces, "You are Peter, and on this rock, I will build my church" (16:18). He then lays out the guidelines for communal relations among Christians, emphasising forgiveness, humility, and obedience to his teachings.

Jesus continues to preach. He forbids divorce and advocates for chastity while elucidating the virtues of asceticism. He warns against the pitfalls of wealth, teaches forgiveness, and welcomes children. In Jerusalem, cheering crowds await him. People spread their cloaks on the road, and others cut branches from the trees and lay them on the path (21:8). Upon his arrival in Jerusalem, Jesus expels the money changers from the Jewish temple and confronts the chief priests and elders, saying, "My house shall be called a house of prayer, but you are making it a den of robbers" (21:13). Jesus's actions earn him the support of the crowds. He admonishes the Jewish leaders, telling them they have been poor stewards of the temple and that the people have been hypocritical, focusing on technical legalities rather than "justice and mercy and faith" (23:23). Observing the wickedness of Jerusalem and foreseeing God's punishment of the wrongdoers, Jesus warns his disciples to prepare for the end of the world. He states that tribulations will precede the final judgment, but the Son of Man—Jesus himself—will come, and the righteous will be saved.

In Chapter 26, Jesus shares the Last Supper with his disciples. He indicates that Judas, one of them, will betray him. Jesus predicts that the other disciples will run away after his death, and Peter will also deny him. As he breaks bread and drinks wine with the disciples, Jesus begins a ritual called the Eucharist, where eating bread and drinking wine symbolise Jesus's body and blood. After having dinner with the apostles, Jesus goes into a garden called Gethsemane. There, he prays, asking God if it's possible to avoid the upcoming suffering. As he leaves the garden, Judas approaches, accompanied by a mob and many Roman soldiers. Judas kisses Jesus to show the angry crowd which man claims to be the Son of God.

Jesus is arrested and brought before the Jewish court, where he is convicted of blasphemy. Caiaphas, the high priest, sends him to Pontius Pilate, the governor of Rome, for a final verdict. Pilate appears surprisingly weak and uncertain. He turns to the crowd for judgment, and they all chant, "Let him be crucified!" (27:22).

Pilate concedes. Jesus is led out, crowned with thorns, mocked, and crucified. On the cross, Jesus cries out, "My God, my God, why have you forsaken me?" before he dies (27:46). Matthew notes the presence of "many women" at the execution, including "Mary Magdalene and Mary the mother of James and Joseph, and the mother of the sons of Zebedee" (27:56). Jesus is buried by Joseph of Arimathea, and a guard is placed over the tomb.

On the first day of the week, three days after the crucifixion, Mary Magdalene and Mary go to visit Jesus's tomb to anoint his body with oils and spices according to Jewish custom, but they find the tomb empty. Astonished, they see an angel who tells them that Jesus has been resurrected from the dead and that he can be found in Galilee. The women leave the tomb both happy and afraid. Suddenly, Jesus greets them and asks them to tell his disciples to meet him in Galilee. After the women go, the guards tell the city's chief priests what has happened, and the priests bribe the guards to report that Jesus's body was stolen while they were sleeping. In Galilee, Jesus commissions his disciples to teach and baptise non-believers as they travel worldwide.

Like all other accounts of Jesus' early life, from birth to death and resurrection, the focus is on his teachings regarding rejection and persecution. However, the most significant aspect for modern-day alcoholics of the Christian faith is their surrender of self-will, the human sacrificial act of offering themselves to God for the sins of humanity. It is the gospel story of his life and the mission he taught, particularly his message at the Last Supper.

Jesus took the bread, blessed it, broke it, and then they ate. He gave it to the disciples and said, 'Take, eat; this is my body.' Then he took a cup, gave thanks, and gave it to them, saying, 'Drink from it, all of you; for this is my blood of the covenant, which is poured out for many for the remission of sins.'

Jesus referred to more than just forgiveness when He said, "This is my body broken for you." He was beaten, mocked, abandoned, stripped, and crucified. He took upon Himself all sin and sickness, as well as humiliation, abandonment, and abuse. Why? So that through faith in Him, we can be reconciled to God and made whole in Him.

Now, here is the rub for alcoholics who believe in Him. In His sacrificial act of dying on the cross, Christians believe that the Spirit of Jesus lives in us. It's a bonus, if you will. We have the resurrected Christ to believe in; His spirit still reigns within our hearts. In some Christian faiths, God is symbolically understood as the Trinity, comprising the Father, the Son, and the Holy Spirit — three divine persons in one Godhead.

Meanwhile, other Christians believe in the spirit of the Risen Christ. Like those who believe in the Trinity, He will come again to save the living and the dead at the end of time. It's enough to say that some of us who accept Jesus as our Saviour have our interpretation, but the assurance that faith in action as an alcoholic provides me gives me solace, allowing me to believe that I have the support I need to believe in and be guided by.

Throughout the Bible, prayer is not merely a suggested activity but a fundamental aspect of a believer's relationship with God. Jesus taught his disciples to pray, emphasising its importance in their lives. The Old Testament is filled with numerous examples of prayer, including the prayers of patriarchs such as Abraham and Isaac, as well as the psalms of King David. These prayers demonstrate the diverse ways people can communicate with God, expressing joy, sorrow, and seeking guidance.

Jesus provided his disciples with a model prayer, known as the Lord's Prayer, which outlines the key elements of a prayerful relationship with God. He also emphasised the importance of persistent and fervent prayer, urging his followers to " ask, seek, and knock."

Turning to the God of your understanding is how we practice our beliefs. It makes sense to realise that despite my character defects, I can use what Christ teaches as a template for remaining sober, one day at a time. So, there it is: living in the Holy Spirit of Christ, who has given Himself to us as a Saviour despite our weaknesses and flawed nature. We should not judge ourselves, but rather continue striving to do God's will in our daily lives and our sobriety, one day at a time.

CHAPTER 4.

A MORAL INVENTORY

We, recovering alcoholics, must remain vigilant to our moral code. Our worship of a higher power is paramount so that it does not become just another form of devotion akin to worshipping people, superheroes, or material possessions. We must look inward at who we are and who we are destined to become. Like all creation, we must have a purpose for living and hoping; without a purpose and a code of ethics to guide us, we would not make spiritual progress, nor would we survive. The Bible text, as dictated by Jesus to his followers, was not a soft sell: " Anyone who wants to be my follower must love me far more than he does his father, mother, wife, children, brothers, or sisters—yes, more than his own life—otherwise he cannot be my disciple."And no one can be my disciple who does not carry his cross and follow me.

In AA Step 4, we are encouraged to search and be fearless in the inventory of ourselves. We have, by instinct, a desire for sex, for material and emotional security and for an essential place in society that often tyrannises us. When out of balance with our natural desires, particularly whilst living an alcoholic life, we have great trouble, practically all the trouble there is.

In our sobriety, we aim to confront the unhappiness we have caused ourselves and others by examining our emotional distortions. We can progress and amend our misguided behaviours. Without a thorough and fearless moral inventory, we soon realise that the faith that works remains out of our grasp. Our flawed nature, which can lead to uncontrollable sexual activity, may jeopardise not only our chances for maturity but also our material and emotional security, as well as our standing in the community. The same principle applies to financial stability when we hoard money instead of utilising it to improve our situation for our family, community, and long-term security. In extreme cases, we might become misers or even recluses, isolating ourselves from family and friends.

Furthermore, the quest for security is not always defined by monetary gain. Some may fear making sound decisions due to an over-reliance on others' guidance and protection. In contrast, others may worry about failing to meet life's responsibilities and disappointing their loved ones. The still-practising alcoholic might feel disillusioned and helpless, once again finding themselves alone and afraid.

Some become insane with power, dedicating themselves to ruling their fellow humans. These individuals often ignore genuine security concerns in favour of maintaining a happy family life. There can be no peace when a person becomes a battleground for instincts. It goes deeper than that; each time the pursuit of wealth tramples over others, anger, jealousy, and revenge are likely to follow. If sexual desire runs unchecked, a similar state of chaos can occur. Excessive demands on others for attention, protection, and love can only lead to domination or rebellion. Such demands only foster unhealthy emotions in those we impose or evoke. In taking stock, we often realise—sometimes unconsciously—that others have instincts too.

Alcoholics often gain insight into the instinctual nature of their behaviours, which is primarily driven by destructive drinking. We drank to drown our fears, frustrations, and depression. We drank to escape guilt and passion, drinking again to cultivate even more love. We drank in vain glory or foolishly inflated dreams, along with feelings of grandeur, pomp, and power. The state of my alcoholism allowed me to bury my regrets and 'sins of omission'; resentments were buried deep, and I needed to free myself from those, too. I needed to confront my anger and thoughts of revenge. In this manner, I thought of Christ saying, "Vengeance is mine." I had to pray and surrender, knowing nothing good would come from my bitterness.

Much of what transpired was serious misgivings on moral grounds, tempered by a Christian upbringing. Still, I could relate to my inherent character defects, embedded in a lifetime of living according to the ways of the world rather than the spirit. If nothing else, this inventory had me recall those hidden things I had buried out of fear. There was much to be done about this alcoholic's former behaviour, and with a sober mind, I could see that progress could only be achieved by applying the first of the steps in my life, too.

The Fourth Step in Alcoholics Anonymous invites members to undertake "a searching and fearless moral inventory of ourselves." This request is not arbitrary; it is essential for establishing a solid foundation for recovery. What this step demands from the member is much deeper and more thorough than anyone may realise at first, but with a bit of diligence and support from a sponsor, the benefits are well worth the effort.

As you may have heard in the program, "first things first." Ensure you are correctly set up to work on your 4th Step by completing the first three steps with another AA member. Only after this initial work in the program can you create a workable 4th Step. There may also be some fear of the 5th Step, in which a member must share the contents of their 4th Step with another individual (ideally their sponsor), which may hinder the process of completing the 4th Step. First, concentrate on thoroughly completing the 4th Step, and then confront your fears about sharing it with someone else.

The Big Book of Alcoholics Anonymous explicitly emphasises the importance of writing down the aspects of the 4th Step on "pen and paper." This inventory cannot and should not be oral. Program members must see their inventory in writing to ensure thoroughness and clarity in their thoughts about themselves and others.

The 4th Step inventory should contain three critical parts: resentments, fears, and sexual conduct or harm done to others.

List any thoughts, experiences, memories, ideas, beliefs, or observations that currently lead to negative emotional or mental experiences. This list may not necessarily include the negative mental or emotional impulses that trigger your drinking. Still, it should consist of the thoughts you harbour that lead to detrimental emotional or mental experiences from the past to the present. Typically, resentments are directed towards a person, object, place, or thing, so having a specific list on paper is crucial for documenting these items. Remember that part of this process involves taking an honest look at any resentments you may have towards yourself, as well as any resentments or reservations you may have about aspects relevant to the program, such as the program itself or a Higher Power.

Listing your fears may feel like an endless task. However, you may be amazed at how they dissipate when you jot them down. Of course, some fears are not as easily removed or identifiable, but that is why you have a sponsor to help you. When considering your fears, some helpful thoughts include asking yourself, "What do I fear today?" Then, move forward and backward and ask yourself, "What do I fear from the past?" and "What do I fear about the future?"

Sexual Behaviour: Depending on your temperament, this section can prove somewhat unnerving. However, experience has shown that sexual conduct is closely linked to our perceptions of ourselves and others. In this light, a thorough exploration of our past sexual conduct, particularly as it relates to uncovering character flaws or blemishes within us, is crucial. Many program members endure long-standing, repressed resentments, shame, and insecurity stemming from past sexual experiences that linger beneath the surface for years. The fourth step involves bringing these lingering fears, worries, shame, and feelings of anger to the forefront for honest examination and reflection. The goal of releasing ourselves from these harmful aspects of our emotional and mental lives makes this process essential and worthwhile.

Righteous Anger: The biggest challenge for those engaging in the first through fourth steps is relinquishing the notion of righteous anger, justifying harmful actions, or rationalising ways that minimise the harm caused. We desire thoroughness and a critical examination of ourselves, which does not excuse the damage we have inflicted on ourselves or others.

When I put pen to paper and began writing my Step 4, I decided to do it my way rather than as outlined in the AA Big Book. I do not suggest that you follow my example to accomplish everything. In particular, if you are in early sobriety, writing your Step 4 is best done with the guidance of a sponsor, following the format on page 65 of the Big Book. I approached it differently due to my thoughts at the time, my business life experiences, and the formality of stocktaking. Consider this method if you struggle to make a list of names: evaluate your wrongdoings toward others and their impact on you due to their flawed nature.

In my detailed template, I first recorded only the names of those I had offended or who had offended me, as I was also aware of a desire for revenge in some instances. I recalled Jesus saying, "Vengeance is mine," so I noted the names of those at the heart of my need to clean the slate and begin anew on my road to recovery. I reasoned that I might forget someone if I paused to assess each person's connection to my resentment, the cause in each instance, and how it impacted me. After all, this was to be a step in my progression through the 12 steps of recovery, and I understood that the next step involved sharing this 4th Step of admission with another person.

The process of recounting my wrongdoings was not new to me, as I had been indoctrinated from a young age to weekly confession in private with a man of the cloth to reconcile myself with God. The outcome was always more a resolution of my sins, more an emotional response than a defective action in my youth. The priest would administer absolution in the name of the Father, Son, and Holy Spirit, and a penance would be given.

In the AA 4th Step process, I listed the names and noted the causes next to each: pride, covetousness, lust, anger, gluttony, envy, or apathy. Once I identified the relevant cause, I examined its effect on my self-esteem, whether it be fear of sexual intimacy, security, or relationships, as it relates to fear of inheritance, to name a few. By taking an honest account of my inherent defects of character, I discovered, like many alcoholics, that much of my spiritual malady was centred around resentment more than any other issue. Therefore, writing it down on paper was a beneficial start to my recovery.

When I stopped drinking, I had to address the consequences of my past alcohol use. Alcohol harmed my relationships, professional life, financial health, and mental well-being. It felt overwhelming and unfair to face responsibilities while working on other aspects of recovery. You notice these feelings arise, indicating that you might benefit from outside support. Leaning on your loved ones or getting professional guidance can help you take attainable steps toward healing and avoid being overwhelmed. Even though I was in the AA programme, I still needed help with my mental obsession. It took two more rehabs in my first ten years of sobriety before I was strong enough to cope without medication. It all came with the guiding help of my AA fellowship, regular meetings, prayer, meditation and putting the steps into my daily life.

I held on to the resentment of losing my family, business and home for a long time. It was not my way to see both sides of the equation for a long time. Dealing with our resentments is integral to achieving sobriety and overall healing. Letting our resentments take up too much space in our thoughts can cause extra stress and trigger us to slip back into old patterns that may include drinking. In addition, focusing on others or situations that cause resentment means we aren't focusing on ourselves, and we can only ever heal and control ourselves. Holding on to negativity towards others only inhibits our growth and healing. Letting go of resentment is part of getting out of our way. We may not be able to rectify all the ways we have been wronged, but we can acknowledge and work through the pain. We have to if we are going to find our way to peace.

Reflecting on my married life and how it had gone awry, I realised the failure was a two-sided affair. When I related it to my drinking, looking at myself through her eyes, I would have left myself, too.

Being aware of resentment is the first step toward managing it. There are several ways to work through resentment, address it thoroughly, and move forward. Resentment and regret often go hand in hand. Sometimes, it helps to recognise how we wish things had played out differently, how we could have shown up differently, and remember that we now have the knowledge to do so.

Resentment often indicates that we are overextending ourselves. Combating alcohol cravings, building healthy habits, and addressing other aspects of recovery can require considerable energy. By caring for ourselves, we can avoid feeling burned out and resentful of the recovery process. Establishing intentional self-care practices, such as meditation, yoga, or reading, will create a ripple effect.

Resentment can also be a sign that your boundaries have been compromised, and it's time to clarify your needs to others. First, pause to validate whatever you're feeling resentful about. Next, recognise the boundaries that could lead to a healthier relationship with the person or experience involved. Such a boundary could be establishing a time limit at family events or keeping a weeknight free to practice self-care. Lastly, practice articulating these boundaries to your loved ones.

You can only control your actions, reactions, and thoughts. As much as we may wish we could control other people's actions, we cannot. Managing our emotional health is a lifelong process that ultimately falls to us. Practising forgiveness and acceptance is easier said than done, but it's necessary for our healing. We must create peace within our lives, and part of that involves accepting the things we can't change. As it says in the Serenity Prayer, "Accept the things we can't change, and have the courage to change the things we can. Do not forget to have 'the wisdom to tell the difference." Reflecting on why someone acts the way they do can help us cultivate compassion and empathy, ultimately leading to a sense of peace. Not only that, but every time we stay in control of our emotions and deal with our pain and anger healthily, we take control of our immediate situation. It's empowering to feel in control of our feelings and behaviours; it just takes patience and practice.

Step Four provided me not only with insight into who I was, but also with an understanding and forgiveness of others. I felt at peace with the process and was eager to move on to Step Five. It took me several years to complete Step Four. The steps are not a race; some take longer than others. In my case, I had to overcome deep depression, quit prescription medications abruptly, and fall into drinking before I found my way back to clarity. It was long after my return to A.A. that I discovered that sharing the message of the Steps with other alcoholics is more effective than anything else. I then attempted to do my 4th Step. The man I chose to share it with has since passed away; there was never a better man than Sam. May he rest in peace, as he was the perfect person for me to share my 4th Step inventory.

Letting go of my ego was a long journey during my early days of sobriety. I had many supportive people around me, but I was so disconnected from my inner spirit that I couldn't see my way past the third step. I did my best to keep surrendering. Then, during my trip through Northern Spain and Ireland in 2017, I thought I had it all sorted. Overall, I had managed to kick my prescription drug addiction cold turkey! I never paid much attention to God or read spiritual books, but, of all things, I drank again.

So, the wake-up call came, and on my return home, I put pen to paper and did my first fourth Step. It was then that I turned to Sam.

CHAPTER 5.

AN ADMISSION TO GOD.

In the New Testament of Christianity, there are two times in the Gospels when Jesus tells people to "go and sin no more." One is after Jesus healed the man by the Pool of Bethesda (John 5:14), and the other is after He rescued the woman caught in adultery from getting stoned to death (John 8:11).

A remarkable blessing of God's gift of salvation is the forgiveness of sins. The forgiven person's past life, no matter what it included, no longer exists. Bridges are burned behind them; gates of yesterday are closed. They are dead to the past. Their life history before becoming a Christian is considered non-existent. They are treated as if the day they became a Christian was the first day of their life.

Through divine forgiveness, man's sins have been washed away (Acts 22:16); he has become as "white as snow" (Isa. 1:18; Psalm. 51:7). His sins have been removed from him " as far as the east is from the west" (Psa. 103:12). His iniquities have been subdued, and his sins have been cast into the depths of the sea. (Micah 7:19.) They have been "blotted out" (LSA. 44:22), "sought for . . . and not found" (Jer. 50:20), cast behind God's back (Isa. 38:17), and when, through an act of God's supernatural gift I reminded of God in Christ entering to my being as a substitute for my former way of living, then it becomes a vital united to Him in my spiritual pathway. It seems like when I enter into Christ, Christ enters into me.

The saving work Christ performed for believers also applies to followers today. In consequence of this vital relationship with Christ, God can justly treat the sinner as if he had done the things that grace did for him. The sinner is treated as if he had obeyed the law's precepts and wanted the law's penalty.

Given the sinner's relation to his God-given grace in the Holy Spirit, God imputes Christ's righteousness to the sinner. Based on this imputed righteousness, which the sinner receives through faith, God, as Judge, declares that the sinner is righteous before the law. He is justified; he is without condemnation.

In Step 5, we admit to God, ourselves, and another human being the exact nature of our wrongs. These AA steps parallel the New Testament view of confessing our wrongdoing and considering making amends, even if it is possible. All the steps require us to go against our natural desires. They are all ego deflation, none more so than Step 5. After so much soul-searching in Step 4 's template of liabilities to my well-being, I was keen to complete Step 5. I had been in AA for ten years when I finally got around to Step 4. I had a plethora of recovering alcoholics that I knew to consider sharing my distressing and past handicaps. It was not as though I had not shared some of the reasons I drank alcoholically with others in the fellowship when asked to share at meetings. Still, the depth of this Step seemed most daunting to me. I soon realised that one of the older sober members was the ideal person to witness my confession of defective habits whilst living an alcoholic life. Sam was a man in his early eighties who had been sober for more than thirty years and had been beside and an adviser to my friend Tony and his wife, who had done Step 5 with him.

So, I met Sam at his home and furnished him with the template layout of my 4th Step. We sat down in the dining room. Sam pulled up another chair next to him, facing me on the opposite side from where I was seated. Before I began my self-appraisal of my defects, I was aware of the need to share from the heart and conceal nothing. Sam began: " Doug, I want you to accept the presence of God and to visualise Him seated in this empty chair. You confess your defect to Him; I am only an observer." It was Sam's wisdom that I now look back upon in this regard, for if I had been sharing with Sam, it would not have been enough. God's presence in that room made me willing to accept this advice and set me on the road to straight thinking, solid honesty, and genuine humility. Once I had finished confessing my past life's wrongs, Sam advised that I take the template of my past life's wrongs, go into the bush, dig a hole, set fire to them, and never look back on them again. So I took Sam's advice and promised to do just that. So Sam boiled the jug and, over a cup of tea, asked me, "Is there anything else?" I replied that there was nothing else to add. Somehow, he had an insight that there was something I hadn't shared, so he asked me again. " Is there something else you haven't shared?' There was a deep-rooted shame I had buried, thinking it better to bury and forget. Sam gently encouraged me to share this deed rooted in shame and fear, and I was relieved from the burden I had carried for over four decades.

It has been several years since Sam died, and he is undoubtedly singing out regularly to the fellowships in heaven. It was not until his funeral ceremony that I learned of his contributions to the government of the day, decision-making, and, in particular, his role in the defence of this country. This man was so humble that he never mentioned his abilities and fame outside of the fellowship of AA. He was kind and gentle, but most of all, he was humble.

I had left Sam and made my way to a bush track. After walking for a while, I entered the land and dug a hole. As Sam instructed, I set a match to my 4th Step template and watched, praying as the smoke rose upward. This was reminiscent of the Jews offering sacrifices to God and of Jesus, who offered his spiritual essence to God as a sacrifice for the sins of humanity.

Once buried, I knew that I was free of all past wrongdoings. i have the feeling of being forgiven. Even more so, there was another dividend from confiding in Sam about my defects of character: it was humbling. It was a sense of knowing what and who I am, followed by a sincere attempt to become whatever God wants me to be. I also recognised on reflection that that solitary self-appraisal, the admission of my defects, was just the beginning, and it would not be enough. Only by holding back nothing, by discussing ourselves with fellow alcoholics in meetings, and by accepting direction and advice from my fellow alcoholics would I have straight thinking. Solid honesty and genuine humility.

In times of trouble, we may ask, "Why can't our God of our understanding tell us where we go astray? He is our Creator, after all, and he gave us our lives in the first place, so why do we need to bring another into it? "Well, it is related to the real test of our willingness to confide and have the confidence to share for accurate self-evaluation. Sharing with others teaches us to listen, too. The way Sam had approached it, with my sharing my 4th Step inventory of self, is the key, for he had me share it not so much with him, but with God. Sam was my counsellor; he kept me on track by asking the right questions and listening to what I was saying to God. He never gave me the answers; God did. I soon realised that my attempts to go it alone in spiritual matters were dangerous. That is why I joined the company of other like-minded fellows who have the same issue through their alcoholism and have done a 4th and 5th Step, and it made all the difference for me. A long-term, older, sober member who understands spirituality is far better to share with, as they possess an inherent spiritual wisdom that one can only learn by listening.

While the Big Book of AA offers guidance for alcoholics striving to live a sober life, immersing ourselves in Jesus's teachings grounds us in his truth. The Bible serves as the most significant evidence regarding Jesus' life, death, and resurrection. Reading the Bible is essential to understand what he said, truly did, and claimed. There, you will discover the meaning of the spiritual— an essence of Christ's sacrifice for humanity and the subsequent benefits bestowed upon us through his grace.

The Gospel writers recorded wherever Jesus went, whom he met, and whatever challenges he faced. They recorded every vital lesson Jesus shared with his closest disciples and the sermons he proclaimed to the enormous crowds that followed him.

At that time, the disciples approached Jesus and asked, "Who is the greatest in the kingdom of heaven?" He called a little child and had him stand among them. Then he told them, "I assure you: Unless you change and become like little children, you will never enter the kingdom of heaven. Whoever embraces this little child is the greatest in the kingdom of heaven." *Matthew 18:1-4*

"The person who is greatest among you will be your servant. Whoever honours himself will be humbled, and whoever humbles himself will be honoured." *Matthew 23:11-12* Some people brought little children to Jesus to have him hold them. But the disciples told the people not to do that. When Jesus saw this, he became irritated. He told them, "Don't stop the children from coming to me. Children like these are part of God's kingdom. I can guarantee this truth: Whoever doesn't receive God's kingdom as a little child receives it will never enter it." *Mark 10:13-15*

Then he [Jesus] poured water into a basin and began to wash the disciples' feet and dry them with the towel he had tied around his waist. When Jesus came to Simon Peter, Peter asked, "Lord, will you wash my feet?" Jesus answered Peter, "You don't know what I'm doing now. You will understand later." Peter told Jesus, "You will never wash my feet." Jesus replied to Peter, "If I don't wash you, you don't belong to me." Simon Peter told Jesus, "Lord, don't wash only my feet. Wash my hands and my head, too!"

After Jesus washed their feet and put on his outer clothes, he took his place at the table again. Then he asked his disciples, "Do you understand what I've done for you? You call me teacher and Lord, and you're right because that's what I am. So if I, your Lord and Teacher, have washed your feet, you must wash each other's feet. I've given you an example to follow. I can guarantee this truth: Enslaved people are not superior to their owners, and messengers are not superior to the people who send them. If you understand all of this, you are blessed whenever you follow my example." *John 13:5-9, 12-17*

We have a long way to go. It is time to stop playing church, realise that judgment is now on us, and turn to God with all our hearts. He promises that if we do this, He will hear from heaven and respond. We must remember that God is the Potter with the power to mould and shape as He wills. As the clay, our job is to yield, realising that even the power to submit comes from Him.

In the New Testament, in four brief verses (1 Timothy 2:1, 3, 4, 6), God states three times that He has planned for the salvation of all. Since He desires to save all men, they must all be given an opportunity. Human experience has shown that very few among all humanity have ever heard revelations of Christ or come to know the truth.

Verse 6 also states that Christ is a ransom for all, which will be testified or witnessed at the appointed time. Paul's phrasing suggests that this testimony is still to come. In other words, many have not heard of Christ's ransom for wrongdoing, and Paul implies that he expects many who are alive at that time, as well as many yet unborn, will also pass away without hearing of it. However, all will witness it at the appointed time because Jesus Christ is the only name under heaven by which people can be saved. At least, this reflects the teachings of the Bible and the testimony that Christians have embraced to the present day, and it is the spiritual essence of many Alcoholics who have found Jesus to be their Higher power.

God's plan, from a human perspective, spans a considerable amount of time. Like Paul, Peter clearly says God does not want anyone to perish. Other scriptures indicate that some will, but it is not God's will that they do so.

The critical factors in these verses are self-condemnation, shame, and guilt. How can a person repent if he does not know the truth, God's purpose, what he should repent for, why he should repent, or how his sins are forgiven? Reconciliation is the essence of Steps 4 and 5.

The real test in Step 5 is to reveal all your story to God and, with the guidance of the one you shared that contrition with, your willingness to confide in whom you share your first accurate self-survey; this is your mission. When your mission is carefully explained to the guide in this situation, it is no doubt apparent to the recipient of your confidence how they can be the conduit to your being free of your burdens; they will be a willing listener.

[Many AA members, once agnostic or atheistic, tell us that it was during this stage of Step Five that they first actually felt the presence of God. Even those who already had faith often become conscious of God and humanity, as they had not been before. This feeling of being at one with God and man, emerging from isolation through the open and honest sharing of our terrible burden of guilt, brings us to a resting place where we may prepare ourselves for the following Steps toward complete and meaningful sobriety.

Self-reflection brings new vision, action, and grace to confront nature's darker aspects. It fosters humility, allowing us to receive God's help. However, this is just the beginning. We desire to nurture the goodness in everyone, even those who struggle the most. But ultimately, we need sunlight; very little can thrive in darkness. Meditation is our way to step into the light.] As Bill sees it, Pg. 10.

"A clear light seems to fall upon us all when we open our eyes. Since our defects cause our blindness, we must first deeply realise what they are. Constructive meditation is the first requirement for each new step into our spiritual growth."

Faith is more than our greatest gift; sharing with others is our most significant responsibility. May we of the AA fellowship continually seek the wisdom and the willingness by which we may well fulfil that immense trust that the Giver of all perfect gifts placed in our hands.

Before proceeding to Step 6: "We entirely ready to have God remove all these defects of character," it is worthy of mention that whilst this book is targeted towards believers in Jesus as a higher power and the essence of the spiritual connection through the Spirit as a consequence of His crucifixion, it should be understood that the embracing of Jesus is not the only acknowledgement of a higher power concept.

At the beginning of AA, atheists and agnostics were part of the fellowship from its founding. Hank Parkhurst, one of the original AA members, was an atheist, and we may not have the Big Book if not for him. Jim Burwell, also one of the early members, was an atheist and is credited with widening the gateway in AA by insisting that the steps read "God as we understand him" or "higher power." Secular AA meetings have been in existence since 1975, and today, they are well-established and widely accepted by the AA fellowship.

I understand that Christian belief is one of many who have a symbolic concept of who God is, whether religious, spiritual or scientific. We should not forget the message that this program embodies. Our primary purpose in AA is to stay sober and to help other alcoholics achieve sobriety. We don't care what they believe or don't believe. Anyone seeking to stop drinking is welcome at an AA meeting, regardless of whether it is secular or not.

However, those of us who understand the spiritual concept of Jesus' message and live according to His Spirit resonate with not just the symbolism of the Risen Christ in a linear, logical way, but also with our creative minds. Our hearts strive to live and act by the message of the Big Book and Christian principles. It is the basis of those who can profess as alcoholics that we are "Alcoholics for Jesus."

As every person has received the gift, so also should they minister the same to one another as good stewards of the manifold grace of God. Every individual has been bestowed with grace-given gifts that were not earned but divinely imparted through God's grace.

CHAPTER 6.

THE GIFT OF RELEASE

The gift of grace offers a chance to start anew. It allows you to be free and to let love flow toward yourself at a deeper level. Understanding grace is essential for letting go. Release what others have done to you, and release what you may have done to others, even unintentionally.

Luke 9:57-62 reveals that Jesus told a person wishing to follow Him that they should be prepared to live without a home (vv. 57–58). He also warned others who wanted to spend time with their families before committing to Him, stating, "No one who puts a hand to the plough and looks back is fit for service in the kingdom of God."

"Whoever wants to be my disciple must deny themselves, take up their cross daily, and follow me" (Matthew 16:24). Jesus made it clear that to be a disciple, one must make a conscious choice to deny everything.

It seems like a tall order to follow Jesus and believe in Him, even if you may not fully grasp the essence of His grace. The message, at least from an alcoholic's perspective, is clear: " Come follow me, and I will make you fishers of men." The 12-step programme of Alcoholics Anonymous is rooted in the principle of surrendering to a God of your understanding, practising the steps, and helping through action rather than just words to assist the still-suffering alcoholic toward sobriety.

The message of Christ Jesus mirrors the plight of those struggling with alcoholism. By grasping his teachings, we can partake in the most profound demonstration of his love. He has endowed suffering with divine significance, rather than viewing it as human absurdity. Thus, human suffering is redeemed. Through our suffering, we engage in Christ's sacrifice, which brings about our salvation and the salvation of others.

As we reflect, meditate, and implement Step 6, we become fully prepared to allow God to remove our shortcomings—defects of character. This is AA's way of expressing that adopting the best possible attitude marks the beginning of a lifelong journey. It does not suggest that we expect our long-standing character defects to be entirely lifted, such as the obsession with drinking. Some defects will persist, but most will be overcome with time. In the meantime, we must practice patience and recognise the improvements.

The journey we undertake in the ways of the spirit is not easy. Once more, I think of St. Paul's letter to the Romans, 7:17-20, which illustrates how difficult it was for him to overcome his flawed nature while preaching God's will in Christ Jesus. I do not understand my actions. Although I want to do what is right, I do what I hate. I recognise that the law is good, even when I act against my will. I no longer commit these acts, but the defects of character that reside within me. I know that nothing good dwells in me; that is, in my sinful nature. I long to do what is good, but I am unable to do so. I do not do the good I wish to do; instead, I keep doing the evil I do not want to do. So, if I act against my will, I am no longer responsible; it is the sin living in me that performs those actions." Then, almost as an afterthought, he says, "But what I do in love, I do unto you."

Nobody says that the path we are on as sober alcoholics is an easy one. However, we should not chastise ourselves but instead get on with it, knowing that our sins (mistakes) are forgiven. As stated in the Big Book of AA, Chapter 4, How It Works, after detailing Steps 1-12, the second paragraph on page 60 states: [Many of us exclaimed, "What an order! I can't go through with it." Do not be discouraged; no one among us has been able to maintain perfect adherence to these principles. We are not saints. The point is that we are willing to grow spiritually. The principles we have established serve as guides to progress. We claim spiritual progress rather than spiritual perfection.]

The AA Big Book states that spiritual life is not merely a theory; we must actively live it. Some wrongs may never be entirely righted. We should not dwell on them if we can correct them. In some cases, there may be valid reasons for postponement, or, as will be discussed in another chapter of this book, it may be better to pray about it rather than make amends face to face, as we may inadvertently reopen a wound in another that is better left alone.

Furthermore, our need for attention must be taken into account when making amends. We should assume that demanding too much attention, protection, and love from others can only invite domination or revulsion. Twelve Steps and Twelve Traditions pg. 44

Examining our relationships involves extracting information about ourselves and our fundamental issues. Since flawed relationships with others have almost always been the immediate cause of our troubles, including our alcoholism, no area of investigation could provide more satisfying and valuable rewards than this one.

Calm, thoughtful reflection upon personal relations can deepen our insight. We can go far beyond what is superficially wrong with us to see the fundamental flaws, flaws that sometimes are responsible for the whole pattern of our lives. Thoroughness, we have found, will pay—and pay handsomely.

Bill Wilson, the co-founder of AA, wrote extensively about seeking guidance from God in surrendering to Him: 'Man is supposed to think and act. He wasn't made in God's image to be an automaton.' 'My formula along this line runs as follows: First, think through every situation pro and con, praying that ego considerations do not influence me. Affirm that I would like to do God's will.'

'Then, having turned the problem over in this fashion and receiving no conclusive or compelling answer, I wait for further guidance, which may come to mind directly or through other people or circumstances. I know if I am wrong, the heavens won't fall. A lesson will be learned, in any case.'

When seeking the message of Christ from the New Testament, we find that he condensed the Ten Commandments, which Moses brought down from the mountain, into two essential steps:" Love God, and your neighbour as yourself." Similarly, Dr. Bob Smith, another co-founder of AA, simplified the twelve steps into three: " Love God, clean house, and help someone. " With such a straightforward philosophy, Dr. Bob helped over 5000 alcoholics maintain sobriety throughout their lives.

While we have completed Steps 4 and 5, we cannot sit on our laurels and assume that no more work has to be done by us. Over many years, we have found that as soon as we think we are in the clear and have peeled back the onion, we discover another layer of defects that must be addressed. Sometimes, we come to a crossroads again and see that the doorway we are trying to get through in our inner spirit is closed. It may be a matter of timing- we are not meant to open certain spiritual doorways until we are ready. We may try many such doorways, but one is always open. It may not be the one we want to enter, but it's best to pursue whatever opportunity arises; you never know where it will lead you on this path to destiny.

We may well recognise that we are powerless, not only over alcoholism but also over people, places, and things. To some degree, we have achieved a certain perfection in letting go of worldly attachments in favour of a spiritual path —living in this world but not being of it. We may have completed Step Five and can practice the previous steps perfectly. While the remaining Steps present ideal standards, we might view this Sixth Step as being in God's hands and do little to ensure perfect progress. We cannot use Step Six as a measure of our progress. Step Six is still challenging, but it is not impossible. The only urgent matter regarding it is that we make a start. We may be entirely ready for God to remove our shortcomings, but it doesn't happen overnight. We must keep working on it. If we are to gain any advantage over our problem beyond alcoholism, we still need to embark on a new journey of open-mindedness. We should adopt a mindset of striving for perfection and be prepared to move forward in our chosen direction. It matters little how hesitantly we walk. The only question is, " Are we ready?"

Still examining our flawed nature, are we willing to set aside our egocentricities and erase the rigid boundaries we have drawn in the past? Perhaps we may say, "This I cannot give up yet...." But we should never tell ourselves, " This I will never give up!" I am reminded once more of Augustine's awareness of the necessity to remove his shortcomings. He prayed, " Lord, make me pure…but not yet." The Bible teaches us that failure is one of God's primary tools for shaping us into becoming more Christ-like. He transforms us through these experiences if we permit Him to do so. Additionally, God sometimes opens new opportunities for us to serve **Him**.

Jesus was unequivocal regarding our problems: ` In this world, we face challenges." (John 16:33). Therefore, problems shouldn't come as a surprise. However, He added: ``But cheer up, I've overcome the world," implying we'll also overcome the world if we do what He says (Romans 8:37, 1 John 5:4-5).

Matthew 7:7-8 encourages us to ask, seek, and knock when looking for solutions to our problems. God promises that those who earnestly seek Him will receive answers, find what they are searching for, and have doors opened to them. We can discover the solutions we need by continually praying and seeking God's help. No one has ever claimed that recovering from failure is easy —a testament to strength. You will regret not trying something far more than you will ever regret trying and failing.

"Christ took humanity and bore the hatred of the world so that He might show men and women that they could live without sin, that their words, their actions, and their spirit might be sanctified to God. We can be perfect Christians if we manifest this power in our lives. When the light of heaven rests upon us continually, we shall represent Christ. The righteousness revealed in His life distinguished Christ from the world and called forth its hatred."

"The word of the Lord, spoken through His servants, is received by many with questionings and fears. And many will defer their obedience to the warning and reproofs given, waiting till every shadow of uncertainty is removed from their minds. The unbelief that demands perfect knowledge will never yield to the evidence God is pleased to give. He requires His people's faith to rest upon the weight of evidence, not perfect knowledge. Those followers of Christ who accept the light that God sends them must obey the voice of God speaking to them when many other voices are crying out against it." 1 John 5:4, 1 Corinthians 15:57, and Romans 10:17.

"Faith is in no sense allied to egocentricity. Only those who have true faith are secure against such arrogance. A puffed-up ego is the dark side of our nature and a counterfeit of faith. Faith claims God's promises and brings forth fruit in obedience. The ego also claims these promises but uses them, as Satan did, to excuse transgression. Faith would have led our first parents to trust God's love and obey His commands. Instead, the ego led them to transgress His law, believing His great love would save them from the consequences of their sin. It is not faith that claims the favour of Heaven without complying with the conditions on which mercy is to be granted. Genuine faith is founded on the promises and provisions of the Scriptures." Hebrews 11:1, Matthew 4:5-7

Let's address what a hazardous open end is. We should strive for perfection; however, some delays might be excused. At the moment of rationalising, an alcoholic might say: "How very easy! Sure, I'll aim for perfection, but I won't rush. Maybe I can indefinitely postpone facing some of my problems." Well, of course, this won't suffice. Such self-deception can overshadow many other pleasant rationalisations. At the very least, we must confront some of our most severe character flaws and take action to address them as quickly as possible.

The moment we say, "No, never!" our minds close to God's grace —this supernatural gift granted to us through the Spirit of Jesus' sacrifice for humanity on the Cross. Delays are perilous, and rebellion can be fatal. Here, we abandon limited objectives and move toward God's will for us.

The foundation for the first six steps of Alcoholics Anonymous (AA), which evolved into the 12 Steps, came from a combination of the Oxford Group, the teachings of William James in "A Variety of Religious Experiences," the insights of Dr. Silkworth, and the experiences of AA's founders, Bill Wilson. During the pioneering period of Alcoholics Anonymous *(before the publication of the Big Book)*, the founders developed a recovery program consisting of six steps. The Twelve Steps, as we know them, originated from Bill's reflections: "Bill went to a place that had been a barrier in his mind and had given him considerable worry. He had to set down the actual program for the alcoholic to follow, and he wanted to make it as robust as possible."

The basic material for the following chapters was the word-of-mouth program Bill had been discussing ever since his recovery. It was heavily influenced by Oxford Group principles and included some ideas Bill had gleaned from William James and Dr Silkworth. Moreover, Bill had worked with Dr.Bob Smith and other alcoholics in testing and sifting the workability and effectiveness of the early program. While he would be the nominal author of the fifth chapter, he was serving as spokesman for all the others.

According to Bill, their word-of-mouth program is a consistent procedure that contains six steps to achieve and maintain sobriety. There is no evidence that the Oxford Group had such a specific program, yet the Oxford Group's ideas pervade in these original six steps, as listed by Bill:

1. We admitted that we were licked and that we were powerless over alcohol.
2. We made a moral inventory of our defects or sins.
3. We confessed or shared our shortcomings with another person in confidence.
4. We made restitution to all those harmed by our drinking.

5. We tried to help other alcoholics without thought of reward in money or prestige.

6. We prayed to whatever God we believed in for the power to practice these precepts.

These original Six Steps correspond to our current Steps: One, Four, Five, Nine, Twelve, and Eleven. Thus, Steps Two, Three, Six, Seven, Eight, and Ten, as we know them today, were added to the program when the Big Book was written.

It was important to Bill that the message of all 12 Steps be adhered to for alcoholics, not only to get what was (is) needed to remain sober a day at a time but also to review progress, make amends wherever possible, meditate and pray regularly, and help the still-suffering alcoholic. It was his way, and the way of the majority of alcoholics, to practice the spiritual aspects of the Steps and therein have a link with the God of our understanding.

It seems we must be brought down to earth before we can rise, endure our discomforts, and surrender to the will of God. This surrender is necessary for progress and for us to be set free. When we experience this spiritual freedom, we become ready to do God's work. We must learn to be humble.

God cultivates humility through the gospel by revealing Christ's humiliation to us. Additionally, He fosters humility through the gospel by highlighting the weight of our sins, disclosing His holiness and grandeur so that we can recognise the darkness of our iniquities.

CHAPTER 7.

HUMILITY

It is interesting to note that in a letter from Bill W to another alcoholic, he wrote of a slightly different version of the first six Steps when he did his inventory with Dr. Bob, AA Co-Founder.

" Dr. Bob had me at the office, and we spent three or four hours formally going through the Six-Step program, as was the case at that time. The six steps were:

1. Complete deflation.
2. Dependence and guidance from a Higher Power.
3. Moral inventory.
4. Confession.
5. Restitution.
6. Continued work with other alcoholics.

Dr. Bob led me through all of these steps. During the moral inventory, he highlighted several of my negative personality traits or character defects, including selfishness, conceit, jealousy, carelessness, intolerance, ill temper, sarcasm, and resentment. We reviewed these at length, and he finally asked me if I wanted these character defects removed. When I said yes, we both knelt at his desk and prayed, each asking to have these defects taken away."

Bill W. was a typical A-type personality: ambitious, aggressive, and competitive. As we may read, Dr. Bob was a typical B-type personality: more relaxed, easygoing, patient, and focused more on the now. It is interesting how God works.

If Bill had his way, the Big Book would have been promoted to the mass market as any author would want. Bob saw it differently; it was a set of suggestions to help the still-suffering alcoholic remain sober. It became a spiritual tool, so to speak, to help us alcoholics stay sober one day at a time, using the guidance of the Big Book. Interestingly, Alcoholics Anonymous, The Big Book, known commonly by members of the AA fellowship, has sold over 30 million copies as of the last recorded date in 2011. In a sense, it is the bible for those of us who suffer from the disease of alcoholism. It is only through the acceptance of a God of our understanding in Step 2 and handing ourselves over to that Higher Power that the spiritual aspects of the 12 Steps come alive in our daily lives, allowing the millions who have followed this path to remain sober.

Let us contemplate this Higher Power. In Christian belief, Jesus sacrificed himself for humanity to atone for humankind's sins and offer a path to reconciliation with God. Christ's sacrifice demonstrated the depth of God's love and provided a means for eternal life.

In Christianity, the Holy Spirit is the third person of the Trinity, co-equal and co-eternal with God the Father and the Son. He represents God's active presence and power among believers. In Christian theology, Christ brings forth the Holy Spirit, the third person of the Trinity, through his death, resurrection, and ascension, fulfilling the promise to send the Spirit as a "Comforter" or "Helper" to guide and empower believers. In his farewell discourse after the Last Supper, Jesus promised his apostles that he would send the Holy Spirit, an "advocate, teacher, and guide," to help them remember his teachings and direct them after his departure.

In Christian celebrations, mainly Catholic, Mass is a reenactment of the Last Supper, when Jesus symbolically explains the celebration of eating the bread and drinking the wine as a representation of his body and blood, thus invoking the Holy Spirit upon the receiver of his sacrifice on the cross. It is a mystery of faith for the believer, just as the expression of invoking a Higher Power is for the alcoholic who doesn't accept Christ's link to the Holy Spirit.

Jesus' final words to the Apostles before his Ascension are: "You will receive power when the Holy Spirit comes upon you, and you will be my witnesses in Jerusalem, throughout Judea and Samaria, and to the ends of the earth" (Acts 1:8). Part 2 of 4: "I will not leave you orphans, I will come to you."

One can hardly blame the apostles, the original followers of Christ, for retreating to that upstairs room in fear of retribution from Roman authorities, who viewed them as collaborators with Jesus. What a surprise it must have been when Christ appeared to them, and they were conscious of the Holy Spirit enflamed in their hearts as they conversed once again with their teacher. Thomas was not there at the time, and when told by the others who witnessed the apparition of Jesus after his resurrection from the dead. Thomas, according to scripture, had remarked: "Unless I see the holes in his hands and the wound in his side, I shall not believe."

The next time Jesus appeared to the Apostles, Thomas was present. Jesus reportedly said, "Thomas, feel the wounds in my hands and side as proof that I am here present." Upon seeing the resurrected Jesus, Thomas immediately exclaimed, "My Lord and my God!" expressing his unwavering belief and acknowledging Jesus's divinity.

Not knowing what to do next, the apostles returned to their occupations as fishermen. At this, the belief comes into play for those of us living today as recovering or recovered alcoholics, apostles becoming fishers of men. Remembering that Christ appeared to them after He had died, we acknowledge that the miracles we believe in as believers in the Spirit of Christ occurred after His death, not while He walked the earth. I speak now of His walking on the water, as seen by those apostles out fishing. The miracle of the casting of nets, as Jesus instructed, by Peter's recall, resulted in the massive fish catch. These and many other miracles are recorded in the New Testament.

We may never be able to prove Christ's spiritual existence outside of the faith that He will return, as mentioned in the Bible. In the meantime, believing in and embracing, at least symbolically, the Holy Spirit will suffice. While the Trinity (God as Father, Son, and Holy Spirit) is a theological concept, its principles can be reflected in everyday human relationships, such as the importance of unity, love, and mutual respect within families, friendships, and our AA communities.

We must also be open to matters of the spirit. In the first version of "There is a Solution," I draw inspiration from Bill Wilson's spiritual experience. Bill Wilson's God is "the Creator of you and me," the "living Creator", and "the living God." He is a God with "a loving and powerful hand", one who is capable of "entering into our hearts and lives" where He can "accomplish those things which by no stretch of the imagination were we humanly capable of."

The Saviour's miracles were "divine acts" as well as "part of the divine teaching" (Bible Dictionary, "Miracles"). Healing and other miracles are still found in Christianity today, though they aren't always dramatic and spoken of publicly because those who experience them hold them sacred. You may want to look for miracles in your life, your family members' lives, or your ancestors' lives. Although we may desire miracles, we should remember that the Heavenly Father answers in His own time and in His way. Miracles are part of the gospel of Jesus Christ. They are a sign that faith is on the earth and a gift of the Spirit.

Whilst we may believe in the spirit of God, one of our modern times was living proof of it. Nikola Tesla was a man ahead of his time. He was a visionary who saw the world in a way that few others did. He was obsessed with unlocking the universe's secrets and believed that the key to doing so lay in the power of nature itself. Tesla believed that the universe was a vast energy source that could be tapped into to unlock the answers to some of life's greatest mysteries. He saw this energy as a way to power the world and create a better future for humanity.

We may seek to improve human conditions through inventions, as Tesla did. Still, it is our responsibility in AA to utilise the Spirit within us all, the Higher Power, if you will, as you may perceive it, for the benefit of our fellow alcoholics.

In our spiritual progress, we must first "humbly ask Him to remove our shortcomings." Step 7 explicitly concerns humility in all we do, for it is the founding principle of all twelve steps.

Humbly ask Him to remove our shortcomings. Step 7 teaches members to be humble, admit their shortcomings, and accept that even their best is not enough to help them overcome their addiction.

Step Seven from the Twelve Steps and Traditions is a collection of Bill W.'s essays on the Steps and the Traditions of Alcoholics Anonymous.

Humility is a key component of A.A.'s recovery program. Often misunderstood, this chapter highlights humility as a necessary aid to survival and an essential antidote to self-centred fear. We should pause here to gain a deeper understanding of what we mean by humility, as it forms the foundation of our spiritual being. Unless we embrace this humility, we will have little left to maintain our sobriety. Furthermore, we have little chance of being truly happy until we become more humble. Without humility, we cannot live with much useful purpose or summon the faith needed to remain sober and assist others in times of human crisis. Humility, both as an ideal and as a word, faces many challenges in our human existence. Not only is the word often misunderstood, but it is frequently met with intentional dislike.

Most human experiences and practices in our world lack humility to an extreme degree. It seems that in today's world, if you want to get ahead, you have to be hard-nosed and aggressive, be a liar and a cheat, make promises you can't deliver, and appeal to the ego of others by displaying narcissistic, egocentric behaviours that others will emulate. (Remind you of anyone you know or admire?). The way things are unfolding out there makes me even more determined than ever to live in this world but not be of it. It has taken a long time for me to come to believe that web alcoholics in our former life were square pegs trying to fit into round holes. If society continues to unfold in this way, what we have in the AA fellowship is a chance to cultivate humility, and if we continue to follow the Steps of AA, we may succeed. And who knows, the world at large might prove to be a better place at any rate. I am darn sure we sober alcoholics will be.

In science and economics, immense resources are being harvested with the promise of a better life ahead. With the material blessings at our disposal, many may believe that an artificial millennium is within our grasp. We have had rash promises that poverty will disappear, abundance will be open to everyone, and personal satisfaction will be desirable. It's a theory that once our primary instincts are satisfied, there won't be much left to quarrel about. The world will turn out to be happy, joyous, and free.

The fellowship of AA makes me more determined to live in this world but not be of the world. We, alcoholics, have always been square pegs who once tried to fit into the round holes of the world. We soon learned with our AA spiritual path that the old ways don't work for us. If we are to be humble, we have to adopt an attitude of gratitude.

We need to learn to make up our minds and adopt the right attitude towards our life circumstances. Abraham Lincoln once said, " We can be as happy as we make up our minds to be." We need to be free. In Jesus' parable, according to biblical interpretation, Jesus advised his followers not to worry about material needs, such as clothing and food, because God would provide for them, just as He provided for the lilies in the fields. Jesus also preached humility in the Parable of the Pharisee and the Tax Collector. The Pharisee stood at the front of the altar and boasted of his charity in giving to people experiencing poverty, fasting, and practising the faith. The tax collector, who in those days was shunned by society, sat at the back of the temple, beating his chest and repeating: " O Lord, be merciful to me, a sinner." Jesus preached about the importance of humility and God's mercy, contrasting the self-righteous Pharisee with the humble tax collector who was justified before God.

Jesus says in Luke verse 14, "I tell you, this man [the tax collector] went down to his house justified rather than the other. Everyone who exalts himself will be humbled, but the one who humbles himself will be exalted." That's the shocking point of it all, for we are asked in Step 7 to ask God to remove our shortcomings humbly — defects of character.

In my ignorance, I suffered much in those early days of my recovery. While diligently following the steps, I never progressed beyond Step three for the first ten years. My logical, linear, half-brain approach gave me what it was all about. Still, I didn't get the essence of Jesus' suffering as I could not relate it beyond my heartfelt pain of loss, despair and deep depression that I had fallen into upon giving up drinking.

It was after that adventure overseas in 2017 when I drank due to being away from the program, but more to the point, not having access to my Higher Power of Jesus in the Spirit. Returning to Australia, I beat depression on that journey, returned to the steps of AA and began to progress from Step 4 through to Step 6 inclusive based on my newfound faith in a manifested Jesus of my creative imagination.

While much of what we say about Jesus may be derived from scripture and historical records of the man, the manifested Jesus is one manifestation of the creative side of our brain in our imagination. It's all symbolic and a heart-to-heart thing, but I didn't understand this until I married the right and left brain as one. Only then did the steps take on a new significance, for it was then, in line with the humble human side of Jesus, that his suffering and death on the cross for all humanity are evident. I could visually depict the sufferings of Jesus through the Steps, and in turn, concentrate more on Christ's sufferings rather than my own. While we alcoholics differ in our beliefs about a Higher Power, mine has always been Christ, instilled in me since childhood and throughout my adult life, both before and after entering AA. Regardless of whether we endured mental or physical torment in our past lives, the truth is that an answer arises when we reflect on the suffering of Jesus Christ. Beginning with his agony in the garden, the scourging at the pillar as ordered by Pontius Pilate, the crowning with thorns, the carrying of the cross up Calvary, and his ultimate agonising crucifixion, such torment was endured for us, for our salvation. It seems appropriate to pause and absorb all this. Viewed on a deeper level, it puts our daily petty hardships, past struggles, and historical sufferings into perspective; often, we inflict our woes of little consequence upon ourselves. In nature, we witness suffering; the life cycle is fraught with pain, and we, too, must endure the slings and arrows of outrageous fortune. We must carry our cross, whether now or in the future.

I am now mindful that much of my writing is a residual parachute in my attempts to fall into the dragon's mouth of my wounded heart. I have escaped it in my writings and songs as I attempt to free-fall into the dragon's mouth without expecting the outcomes. The steps help. Step seven certainly helps me focus on the humility that Jesus embraced, and in turn, I am encouraged to overcome my character defects. We have demanded more than our share of security, prestige, and romance for thousands of years. When we seem to be succeeding, we drink to dream even more fantastic visions. When we are frustrated, even to some extent, we often turn to drinking ourselves into oblivion. Never was there enough of what we thought we wanted. In all our strivings, many of them well-intentioned, our crippling handicap has been our lack of humility. We lacked the perspective that character-building and spiritual values must come first and that material satisfaction is not the purpose of living. Quite characteristically, we have confused the ends with the means. Instead of considering the satisfaction of our material desires as a means of living and functioning as human beings, we thought these satisfactions to be life's ends and aims. It requires acknowledging that one cannot do everything alone and recognising the need for external help, whether from a higher power, the community, or a support system.

Recognising faults and deciding to get sober, those who complete this step embrace humility. Humility is freedom from pride or arrogance: the quality or state of humility. By definition, humility is the very thing many alcoholics and addicts have been missing throughout the entirety of their addiction. We are to acknowledge God, in Jesus' spirit, humbly and with a contrite heart, asking Him to lead us in all our thoughts, words and deeds as we go about our daily lives. The solution to our problem is what spiritual progress is all about.

In our amendment process, we demonstrate the difference between how we behaved before and how we will act after making amends in each case. In this step, we try to figure out why the problem has developed, which is an essential part of the "problem-solving process" to guarantee the proper responses from ourselves and help others "own" their share of the problem.

CHAPTER 8.

MORE ON MAKING AMENDS

Whilst the purpose of making restitution to others is paramount, it is equally necessary that we extricate from an examination of our relations every bit of information about ourselves and our fundamental difficulties that we can see since defective relations with other human beings have nearly always been the immediate cause of our woes, including our alcoholism, no field of investigation could yield more satisfying and valuable rewards than this one. Calm, thoughtful reflection upon personal relations can deepen our insight.

We can look beyond what is superficially wrong with us to uncover the fundamental flaws that can sometimes drive the entire pattern of our lives. We have discovered that thoroughness pays off—and pays off handsomely.

We may ask what harm we did to others and ask for forgiveness. In other cases, we may ask what damage was done to us, and as hard as that may be to accept, we need to forgive them, too, despite the depth of the agony. " Father, forgive them, for they know not what they do." We must define harm practically. We may call it instinct when it collides with other internal feelings that cause physical, mental, or spiritual damage to others and ourselves.

When it comes to our misbehaviours, it may not be a complete catalogue of our past defective actions and the harm we may have caused. We must not forget the subtle ones that can be just as damaging, such as being tight with money or being irresponsible, callous, and cold-hearted. We may be irritable, critical, and impatient.

In the Alcoholics Anonymous (AA) Big Book, Steps 8 and 9 involve making a list of all the people you have harmed and developing a willingness to make amends to them. These steps are crucial in the 12-step process, focusing on acknowledging the impact of your actions and taking responsibility for past wrongs. Here, we revisit Step 4 and create a list of all individuals we have harmed, to be open to making amends to them all. The path toward renewal and personal growth in recovery is a gradual process. The 12-step program of Alcoholics Anonymous provides a framework to slowly but surely achieve this new mindset. In compiling this list, we ask our higher power to help us acknowledge our wrongdoings towards others. We are also seeking God's forgiveness for others and ourselves. "Lord Jesus, in your Spirit, grant me the willingness to begin my restitution in the forgiveness of the wrongs I have done."

The Serenity Prayer is the most well-known AA prayer, often recited at the beginning and end of each 12-step meeting. "God, grant me the serenity to accept the things I cannot change, the courage to change the things I can, and the wisdom to know the difference."

We may also create a list again of all individuals we have harmed, define our challenges in addressing our amends, clarify the issues, outline our goals for what we hope to achieve, identify the root causes of these issues, develop an action plan, and carry out the necessary actions. Once completed, we evaluate the results, continuously focusing on future improvement. We should categorise the list into three groups: people we may not wish to make amends to, those we might eventually make amends to, and those we cannot envision ever making amends to.

In essence, we learn about the 8-step process, which includes clarifying the problem, containment, analysing and breaking it down, target setting, analysing the root cause(s), developing and planning countermeasures, confirming the results, and standardising and sharing. Just as recognising and acknowledging our utter failure in the face of character defects is a prerequisite to transforming our lives in the AA progression of the Steps, a deep consciousness of our frailty is required to pursue overcoming and growth by following Jesus's spiritual way and glorifying Him. All these defective characteristics can be just as damaging to others as what may seem to be more serious defects in our eyes.

The root cause of our defective characteristics was uprooted in step 8 when we "Made a list of all persons we had harmed and became willing to make amends to them all." We, by intention, take action to right past wrongs with a contrite and humble heart; the miracle of conscious contact with God is set into motion. By adopting the spirit of Jesus, we, though weak in our character, become strong in faith and enhance our spiritual approach to living the Steps of AA.
Once we've reviewed all aspects of human relations and identified which personality traits have caused harm or upset to others, we then begin to delve into memories of those we've offended. It's usually easy to remember those most affected. Yet, over time, a long list of individuals may emerge who have been impacted by our behaviour. We should reflect on each case carefully and be willing to make amends whenever possible. Once we've cleared our conscience, so to speak, we will feel lighter, aware that other AAs have gone through the same soul-searching process and that we are one step closer to connecting with our fellows and with God.

The exercise did not seem as difficult as one might expect. While my viewpoint here is a distinctly Catholic perspective rather than a Christian account, it serves to highlight the way of making amends, expressing sorrow, and reflecting on one's wrongdoing in prayer. [As a child and in my teens, I had a weekly ritual of reflecting on my defective nature in dealing with others. We participated in confessionals with a priest, starting with an opening prayer: "Bless me, Father, for I have sinned. It has been seven days since my last confession. I have said the Confiteor [a prayer of confession in Latin involving the spirit of God, the Virgin Mary, Archangel Michael, apostles Peter and Paul], and these are my sins." The prayer ends with "Through my fault, my fault, my (own) grievous fault." One would then recount all the mistakes made during the week. The priest listened and offered an absolution blessing: "I absolve you from your sins, in the name of the Father, Son, and Holy Spirit." He would then assign a penance, such as three Hail Mary's and the Glory be to the Father prayer, before giving a sign of the Cross blessing. The old version of the Confiteor included a more detailed list, reminiscent of Step 4 or Step 8, sharing the same core message of acknowledging sin and asking for forgiveness for those we had offended.]

Thus, the habit of making amends was not new to me; however, the Step 9 instruction, "Made direct amends to such people wherever possible, except when to do so would injure them or others," did not factor in. It was understood that once one confessed and completed a penance, one could release the need to address those offended face-to-face.

"The readiness to take the full consequences of our past acts, and to take responsibility for the well-being of others at the

same time, is the very spirit of Step Nine."– Twelve Steps and Twelve Traditions, p. 83

At this point in our step work, we may be trudging the road to a happy destiny, but we've reached the point where we must repair what we left behind on a path of shattered relationships. As active addicts and alcoholics, we likely lied, cheated, or stole to get, use (and hide using) our drug of choice… because addiction creates absolute moral wreckage.

Step 9 of AA Alcoholics Anonymous is the perfect time to let go of the horrible way we feel about our past and to repair relationships radically. In my experience, walking around with the weight of amends that need to be taken care of really sucks. More importantly, living with the leftover guilt and shame from past wrongdoings prevents us from moving forward and puts us at risk of using again!

You've probably already discovered that by staying clean and sober and by working the Twelve Steps of AA, things are getting better. That's because *we are* getting better. Becoming a "better person" means we are less willing to engage in destructive behaviours, mainly because we know how much they cost us in human misery. An awareness of other people replaces that self-centeredness, and instead of being indifferent, we begin to care. Where we were selfish, we began to be selfless. When we are angry, we tend to become more forgiving.

So, what is Step Nine of AA Alcoholics Anonymous? Step Nine is that significant step we likely created some anxiety over because it involves making amends. We should make direct amends to those we have harmed whenever possible. What does that mean? There are three kinds of amends: we make direct amends by taking personal responsibility for our actions to the person we wish to reconcile with. Then, there are indirect amends, such as finding ways to repair damage that cannot be reversed or undone by volunteering and helping others. Lastly, living amends involves demonstrating to others that you've made a genuine lifestyle change and are committing to yourself and those you've harmed by discarding your previous destructive behaviours.

We have already begun making amends to ourselves by changing some of our behaviours, attitudes, and beliefs. The part of the amends process where we change ourselves impacts everyone around us and continues long after we've spoken directly to someone we have harmed. When making amends to others, many fears and expectations usually arise. We may fear making financial amends or worry about rejection, retaliation, and other uncertain outcomes. However, making amends doesn't always have to be a nerve-racking, dreadful, or joyless experience. You might also feel excited about possibly healing a relationship or happily anticipating the relief you will feel after making a particularly daunting amendment or paying off a debt. Freedom is achieved by tidying up the past, allowing you to live peacefully in the present.

To keep things as straightforward as possible, focus on the purpose of the Ninth Step. Remember the concepts known as "The Three R's" of the Ninth Step related to making amends: Restoration—bringing something back to its former state. The outcome may involve restoring our reputation or even a relationship. Resolution, as a recovering alcoholic, signifies that we likely have past experiences that disturb us in some way. Finding a solution means uncovering answers to resolve these matters. Restitution is the final aspect linked to the Ninth Step: returning something of material or abstract significance to its rightful owner.

Even though we may be eager to rip the Band-Aid off and quickly complete an amendment, we must avoid being impulsive or careless. Thought and planning are necessary to achieve the best possible outcome. Conversely, it is equally important not to procrastinate in making amends. Why? Based on experience, many recovering individuals have relapsed when they allowed their fears to prevent them from doing Step Nine. Dr. Bob, one of our founders, could not stay sober until he went around town and made amends to all those he had hurt.

As with our previous steps, it's essential to be realistic: Completing your Ninth Step cannot be neatly contained within a specific time frame. We don't finish our Eighth Step list and then immediately start marking off "completed" amends like we would for items on a shopping list. Some of our amends may never be fully resolved, and our efforts may continue throughout our recovery. The truth is that every day, we make an effort to refrain from hurting our families, friends, coworkers, and even strangers, and strive to practice loving behaviour with them. It's a day when we've continued our amends. Even seemingly concrete amends aren't necessarily completed once we have addressed a matter, such as paying off debt. Continuing to pay off debts and refraining from lying, stealing, or cheating will be an ongoing part of the Ninth Step practice.

Life is complicated and not always straightforward or black and white. Therefore, some Step Nine amendments require creativity and patience. Working through these steps should never lead to further harm to others. There may be times when approaching another person directly or seeking to provide restitution could be painful or harmful for that individual. For example, there may be situations where the person (or people) we've harmed are unaware of our actions, and learning about them might cause additional pain. Alternatively, situations could be complicated by other addicts or accusations beyond mere financial theft. Many types of situations exist, and each must be carefully considered individually. Once again, our sponsor can help us determine the best course of action for each case. They can assist us in evaluating our motives for wanting to disclose our addiction or apologise. You may want to ask yourself if that person needs to know, and if so, what purpose would be served by sharing such information.

If we approach our amends list openly while discussing it with our sponsors, we can consider these situations in ways we haven't previously contemplated. We often find that what we initially considered the apparent method of making amends might not be the best approach.

Humility is freedom from pride or arrogance, and in the Ninth Step, we will focus on the spiritual principles of humility, forgiveness, and love.

We gain humility by reflecting on the harm we have caused to others (and ourselves) and by accepting responsibility for our actions. After acknowledging what we have done, we take steps to make it right. There is nothing quite like experiencing increased humility while making amends in your Ninth Step, recognising the self-empowerment and self-love that accompany it.

While making amends and experiencing forgiveness, we come to understand the value of extending it to others. It feels good to practice forgiveness and let go of resentment! Positive reinforcement is a powerful motivator for practising the spiritual principle of forgiveness as much as possible. Forgiving others allows us to recognise our humanness, making us less judgmental than we were before. We become aware that since we usually mean well, we can extend that belief to others. It's interesting to note that when someone harms us, holding onto resentments only robs us of our peace and serenity, prompting us to forgive them sooner rather than later. It's worthwhile.

Practising the spiritual principle of love has been an integral part of our recovery and maintaining our sobriety. By Step Nine, we've eliminated many destructive attitudes, perspectives, and feelings we once held, creating space for love in our lives. As we become filled with love, we need to share it by nurturing our existing relationships, building new ones, and selflessly sharing our time, resources, and recovery experiences with those who need them.

Guilt and shame are unnecessary burdens that tether us to our past. By practising these spiritual principles, we can break free from these burdens and achieve the freedom from the addiction we have longed for. I'm sure you've heard that the steps are written in a specific order for a reason. Each step provides the spiritual preparation we need for the subsequent steps. Never in a million years did we imagine during our drinking days that we would one day be able to sit down with the people we've harmed and make direct amends! The spiritual guidance from one's higher power would not have been attainable without the spiritual preparation we received from the previous steps.

Without completing the work in the first eight steps, we wouldn't have a foundation to stand on while making our amends. Without a relationship with a Higher Power, we wouldn't possess the faith and trust necessary to tackle Step Nine! Had we not finished our Fourth and Fifth Steps, we might still be unclear about our responsibilities and would lack the clarity needed to understand what we were making amends for. If we hadn't developed humility through the Sixth and Seventh Steps, we'd likely approach our amends with self-righteousness, blame, or anger. Our Eighth Step list served as practical preparation for working on Step Nine. As we proceed with this step, it is essential to remain connected to a Higher Power and to believe that the previous eight steps have adequately prepared us to work on the Ninth Step.

Do you want to be free? There are no half-measures, and it isn't easy. If it were easy, everyone would be doing it! It takes strength and courage to acknowledge our mistakes and restate when necessary. Our actions in this humility are another rewarding part of our recovery journey, bringing us closer to the gift of freedom. Many of us find it helpful to reflect on our amends after making each one. Some of us do this by writing about how it felt to make amends and what we learned from the experience.

Living our Ninth Step requires avoiding new debts, wrongdoings, or misdeeds. Preventing such future liabilities is as essential to our amends process as regular payments on past debts. "Freedom" seems to encapsulate the essence of Step Nine. It represents the relief from guilt and shame, the reduction of our obsession with "self," and the increased ability to appreciate what's happening around us. We may begin to view our past as a treasure trove of experiences to share with those we aim to help in recovery, rather than as a period of darkness we regret. We stop measuring our lives by what we lack and start to recognise the gifts we receive daily. Above all, we understand that to uphold this feeling of freedom, we must continually apply what we've learned while working through the steps, one day at a time. Through this practice, we gain a new perspective, and the promises of the Ninth Step become a reality in our lives. Sometimes quickly, sometimes slowly.

CHAPTER 9.
AWARENESS IN SPIRIT

Step 10 in AA is frequently summarised as "Continued to take personal inventory and when we were wrong, promptly admitted it." The purpose of Step 10 is to encourage self-awareness, accountability, and continuous personal growth for individuals in alcohol addiction recovery.

Continuing to engage in our daily activities usually means improving at them. This principle applies to Step 10 of Alcoholics Anonymous. Nobody truly enjoys admitting to being wrong; it's much easier to place blame on others. Acknowledging our mistakes and being accountable for our actions are essential for maintaining our spiritual progress during recovery. The best aspect of practising the Tenth Step of AA in our daily lives is that the more we engage in self-discovery, honesty, humility, and reflection, the fewer apologies and amends we need to make!

Taking a personal "inventory" in Step Ten involves assessing our emotional disturbances, particularly those that might lead us back to drinking.

As it says in The Big Book, when we are disturbed, it is more often than not because we find some person, place, thing or situation – some fact in our lives – unacceptable. A typical response to disturbance is *blaming* our feelings and reactions on others. Alcoholics and addicts have typically honed the skill of nursing resentments and finding fault into an art form! We tend to give others control over our lives when we say they "make us" angry, upset or afraid. The reality is that we often say or do something that contributes to creating these conflicts in our lives. Step Ten of Alcoholics Anonymous suggests that it is time we take responsibility for our actions and promptly clean up our role in all matters. Our actions require us to be willing to release selfishness, dishonesty, resentment, or fear when they arise. Step Ten of AA puts into practice the spiritual principles of vigilance, maintenance and perseverance.

Acknowledging what's working and balanced can also help us to pinpoint what's out of balance and *not* working. Continuing to take personal inventory isn't only about finding out when we are wrong; however, because we can't identify the times when we are wrong unless we have also identified the times when we have handled things "rightly" as a basis for comparison.

Self-discipline & perseverance are almost counterintuitive for us addicted to alcohol. When we were using alcohol, we were probably self-seeking and self-absorbed, always taking the easy way out, giving in to our impulses, and ignoring any opportunities for personal growth. The self-discipline required for recovery calls on us to do certain things regardless of how we feel. For example, we must attend regular meetings, even if we're tired, busy at work or play, or feeling filled with despair. We go to meetings, call our sponsor, work with others and practice spiritual principles because we have decided we want recovery in AA. Those actions are essential to help ensure our continued recovery.

The principle of integrity in AA can be complex, as sticking to commitments and keeping our word is only a tiny part. Integrity in recovery is the art of knowing which principles to practice in any given situation and in what measure.

Most of us discovered, upon sobering up, that we had never been able to maintain any long-term relationship, certainly not one in which we resolved our conflicts in a healthy and mutually respectful manner. Whether it was raging fights with people who never spoke of the underlying problem that caused the fights, or not standing up for ourselves and being conflict-avoidant because it seemed easier to burn a bridge rather than work through a problem and build a stronger relationship. These are all parts of continuing to take inventory to reveal our most outstanding liabilities and assets. Let's expand on that.

Step Ten emphasises the need to continue taking personal inventory and asserts that we do this solely to discover when we're wrong. But how can we identify the wrong times unless we also have the correct times as a basis for comparison? Identifying the moments we do things right and forming personal values are just as integral to personal inventory as recognising our liabilities.

The Tenth Step reminds us to admit when we are wrong promptly, but this assumes that we always recognise our mistakes! The truth is that most of us do not, at least not immediately. By taking a personal inventory, we can better identify when we are at fault. We use Step Ten to maintain ongoing awareness of our feelings, thoughts, and, even more importantly, what we are doing.

Have you ever noticed how much thought and feeling are tied to our actions? It's genuinely intriguing. For instance, many of us struggle with anger; we dislike how it affects us. We might judge it, convince ourselves we have no right to feel this way, and then do our utmost to suppress it. Yet, we may find ourselves in situations that provoke anger in anyone, and when we reflect on this, we begin to feel uncomfortable. Then comes the moment when our recovery can either propel us forward into greater self-respect or drag us down into a thick fog of depression and resentment. It all hinges on how we respond to our thoughts and feelings of anger. If we scream, curse, and throw things, we diminish any chance of improving a relationship, job, or situation. Conversely, if we do nothing and bury our feelings, we risk becoming depressed and resentful, which also doesn't enhance our circumstances. If we take constructive action to improve the situation, we increase the chances of a positive outcome, or at the very least, we will recognise when it's time to walk away and be able to do so without regrets.

It's unproductive to list our feelings or become aware of them without connecting them to the specific actions they provoke or, in some instances, fail to provoke. Before starting a regular practice of personal inventory, it is crucial to understand what we are evaluating in that inventory.

It is a complete myth that Step 10 of AA is about constantly needing to apologise to everyone. Some people get hung up on this step, which requires admitting when you've done something wrong. However, it's less about apologising to others and more about being aware of the thoughts, feelings, words, and actions that can harm yourself and others. It is a very personal process of continual inward reflection.

And here's the truth: You will undoubtedly continue to make mistakes as you interact with others! However, a commitment to Step 10 is to take personal responsibility for your mistakes. By examining your thoughts and actions each day and addressing them, negative thoughts and feelings will not escalate to the point where they threaten your recovery. You can trust your progress and know that practice and patience will ensure continued recovery.

Examining our conscience, we focus on where we have gone astray while maintaining constant contact with our Higher Power. For those of us who believe that this represents the spiritual essence of Jesus in our hearts today, it makes the process even more interesting and easier to come to terms with when we hand it all over to Him.

However, sometimes we may wonder why we put ourselves through all this introspection, recalling grief and suffering, if we have already acknowledged that we alcoholics have a Higher Power to turn to. In Step 3, we surrender our all in the faith that the God of our understanding will guide us. Should that not be enough? Can't we let the past go in faith, trusting that God will set us free?

Making amends for past indiscretions enables healing for both the person who caused harm and the person who was harmed, as it involves acknowledging responsibility, taking action to repair the damage, and fostering reconciliation and forgiveness. Making amends demonstrates accountability for past actions, which can be a decisive step toward self-awareness and personal growth. It offers a chance for the harmed person to heal emotionally and for relationships to mend, fostering forgiveness and rebuilding trust. Acknowledging mistakes and taking steps to rectify them can alleviate the guilt and shame associated with past behaviours, allowing for a sense of closure and a path forward. Making amends goes beyond a simple apology; it involves acting to right the wrong and restore balance with the other person. Such a process can help repair relationships.

Making amends can be a valuable opportunity for personal growth and development. It allows individuals to learn from their mistakes and develop stronger empathy and responsibility. By acknowledging past wrongs and taking steps to repair them, individuals can move forward with a clearer conscience and a stronger sense of integrity.

As it says in "As Bill Sees It" on page 222:" We finally saw that the inventory should be ours, not the other man's. So we admitted our wrongs honestly and became willing to set these matters straight."

So, for the moment, while on the subject of introspection, I want to examine a little more the handing over to God—the symbolism, the essence of that Higher Power that we have come to believe in and depend upon to remain sober a day at a time and live a spiritual life rather than a worldly one.

A living example of one who acknowledges God in the face of being constantly in the public eye as the icon of all poetic and musical artistry is Bob Dylan. Long before he became a legend in his lifetime, he was known by his real name, Robert Allen Zimmerman, a Jewish boy from the iron mining town of Hibbing, Minnesota. He taught himself to play the piano and guitar and spent only one year at university before dropping out to pursue his life's work as a singer-songwriter and author, ultimately being recognised by winning a Nobel Prize in Literature.

He decided to change his name to gain some anonymity on stage. He believed that by adopting a new name, he could transform into an entirely different character while performing, and that transformation has long contributed to the singer-songwriter's lasting appeal.

However, what I seek to impart here is not his creative talent but his experience with faith in God and his examination of that faith in action. To do this, it is not unfair to examine the times of his younger career and the influences upon him at the time, which caused him to embrace Christianity for a time, in preference to returning to his Jewish faith and the roots of childhood indoctrination. It was in the 1960s and early 70s of the Vietnam War that singers, songwriters and artists of the time sang protest songs against the war, marched to stop the bombings in the killing fields and marched for civil rights and the freedom of the people. None was more present in these causes than Bob Dylan.

The Haight-Ashbury neighbourhood of San Francisco, particularly in the 1960s, became the centre of the counterculture movement associated with the Hippie Movement, based on the ideals of free love, drugs, and music. It was the mecca of revolutionaries, famous singers, and a community whose ideals spread far and wide at the time. During the 1960s, the assassinations of John F. Kennedy, Martin Luther King Jr., Robert Kennedy, and Malcolm X, alongside the National Socialism embedded in government controls, saw the movement fade. People became disillusioned with the Hippie Movement and the philosophies of counterculture and revolutionaries, seeking a new way and looking to embrace a new belief.

Then, Moishe Rosen, an Orthodox Jew by birth, began to follow Jesus, became a Baptist minister, and arrived in Haight Ashbury after being dismissed from the American Board of Missions to the Jews due to his evangelistic preaching methods. In 1973, we founded a new Baptist church that preached Jesus' doctrine to Jews, primarily focusing on individuals of Jewish ancestry. The organisation is linked to Messianic Judaism, which integrates Jewish practices with Christian beliefs, including the conviction that Jesus is the Jewish Messiah.

Bob Dylan didn't buy into any of this and initially remained aloof. He announced in 1971, "I am a Jew. It touches my poetry and life in ways I can't describe." While the Jewish movement for Jesus attracted many Jews from all walks of life during the mid-to-late 1970s, it wasn't until 1978 that Bob Dylan publicly embraced it. At a 1978 concert in San Diego, towards the end of a long tour, he was ill and struggling with the emotional devastation of divorce. Someone threw a small crucifix onto the stage at the end of a set of songs. Dylan picked it up and put it in his pocket. He experienced a profound religious encounter in a Tucson hotel room, describing it as the physical presence of Jesus. The experience led to his embrace of Christianity, after which he wrote and recorded a series of gospel albums. He said then, "Jesus put his hands on me." He had various biographies and similar accounts, and it seems he did not enter Christianity through AA: he was fried from amphetamines during the electric era (c. 1964-1966) and coked out during Rolling Thunder as his divorce unfolded (c. 1974-1976). However, he was also soaked in booze during his career low in the mid-eighties following his conversion.

He faced the wrath of fans during the '60s electric era. One fan booed and shouted, "Judas!" at him. He responded into the microphone, "You don't mean that." A pivotal moment for Dylan was his realisation that fans viewed him as messianic. They emphasised his Judaism as a marker of divine prophecy, which made him very uncomfortable. This messianic title may have distanced him from his traditional Jewish identity, which he was already downplaying in favour of his raconteur persona, even though the press's first act in the early '60s was to identify him by his birth name, Zimmerman, and endlessly discuss it. Further complicating Dylan's religious identity is his Jews for Jesus-esque approach to merging his birth identity with his evangelism. He celebrated

He performed at his children's Bar Mitzvahs and Chabad (Orthodox Jewish) fundraisers on New York-area cable in the '80s. Such a change is not uncommon for a Jewish-born evangelical Christian, but it can confuse gentile onlookers.

Aside from his ' Gospel concerts', Dylan held several shows addressing the excesses of smoking, drinking, and coffee. Reportedly, he quit drinking alcohol in 1994, and those close to him observed a significant change in his behaviour afterwards. While he never explicitly discussed his addiction or recovery.

During those years, from 1979 to 1981, the king of counter-culture became a born-again Christian, and his output reflected this shift. I wouldn't say, "he found God," for he already had God. Raised in a Jewish household in the American Midwest, he underwent the religious ritual of a bar mitzvah at the age of 13 and attended Jewish summer camps. However, he kept his faith hidden in his professional life and, more than anyone, seemed to epitomise the Sixties culture that largely rejected religion. Born again, he completed a three-month Christian study course and was reportedly baptised, though the evidence is limited. His songwriting and concert performances reflected his newfound faith, but fans and critics remained unimpressed. The opening night of a Dylan tour in San Francisco in November 1979 received a memorably scathing review in the San Francisco Chronicle, where the critic wrote: "Dylan has written some of the most banal, uninspired, and uninventive songs of his career during his Jesus phase." The headline read: "Bob Dylan's God-Awful Gospel."

So, for those of us who see Dylan in concert today and are fortunate enough to hear him speak even a single word, the performances showcase the singer engaging with his audience during this period. Except he doesn't so much talk as preach. At one concert, the man who now struggles to say "Hell," "Goodnight," or "Thank you" on stage told a stunned audience: "You know we're living in the end times ... The scriptures say, 'In the last days, perilous times shall be at hand. Men shall become lovers of themselves. Blasphemous, heavy, and high-minded... Take a look at the Middle East. We're heading for a war. I told you 'The Times They Are A-Changin'" and they did. I said the answer was 'Blowin' in the Wind, ' and it was. I'm telling you now that Jesus is coming back, and He is! And there is no other way of salvation. Jesus is returning to set up His kingdom in Jerusalem for a thousand years."

So, please excuse me for devoting so much time to folk hero Bob Dylan. My point is that, symbolically, he embraced Jesus as his Saviour (Step 2), allowed him to enter and influence his life (Step 3), and wrote his lyrical songs as if he were doing Step 4. He certainly has not wasted his time guiding the masses. Followers armed with truth, facts, and a vision for the future- is it not our duty to use our talents as God intended us to? As a Jew, Dylan was given the symbol of a crucified Christ, who acted for the betterment of humanity. Unlike most, he was fortunate to sense Jesus's presence, whom he described as laying his hands upon him. Those who need change are often blessed with unique gifts that enable them to help others. St. Paul, the evangelist in the Bible, is perhaps the best example. Indeed, in our fellowship of AA, Bill Wilson had a flawed nature, yet accomplished so much for the benefit of us alcoholics during his lifetime that continues to resonate to this day.

CHAPTER 10.

SPIRITUAL GUIDANCE

Through Step 11, we learn that we establish conscious contact with God through prayer and the mediation of spiritual guidance.

In everyday life, "handing over" to a higher power can represent trusting in something beyond oneself for guidance and support, whether through prayer, meditation, or simply recognising one's limitations and seeking help when needed.

You must work with God. Surrendering doesn't mean turning your life over or relinquishing control; it means accepting your life as it is. It involves accepting help and trusting that a power greater than yourself will lead you in the right direction. Trust that God will guide you to a better life.

As I have previously indicated, while I am more inclined to promote the virtues of Jesus in Spirit as a Higher Power or the theological concept of a Trinity of Father, Son, and Holy Spirit- demonstrating unity in diversity and mutual love, as seen in family dynamics or collaborative efforts- AA is not confined to a religious deity but can be anything an individual considers to be of greater power or influence than themselves. Some examples of a higher power in AA include a religious or spiritual entity, such as God, Allah, or Buddha, as well as the collective wisdom of the AA group.

Prayer and meditation weren't easy when my world turned pear-shaped. It was not for the lack of trying, as I prayed and attended various religious services, meditation groups and chakra methodologies, sweat lodges, Thai massages, drawing feelings in the sand, barefoot meditation focusing on the sensation of the earth beneath my feet, relationships with a woman when I should have gone to

God, and adventures on many long pilgrimages. In the end, nothing worked as effectively as rest, recuperation, and turning my will over to a God of my understanding, using the AA Steps as a template to work on my spiritual path. I recognised that I belonged to the one to three per cent of the population who are alcoholics, and I was advised to let this soak into the marrow of my bones. A mentor in rehabilitation taught me to set my personality on the spiritual waters of life and to trim my sail to stay on course. He followed Jung's views on spirituality and suggested I go with the flow; all I needed to do to stay on course was touch the rudder now and then. He was a retired psychiatrist, an alcoholic like me, and a fellow patient dealing with depression and anxiety after long-term sobriety. At that point, I did not know that I would undergo three rehabs over the next decade in Alcoholics Anonymous before the message would genuinely sink in. Only after walking the Camino de Santiago for the third time did the AA Steps resonate with me, making handing over to the Spirit and complete surrender effective.

It was then that the second message from my mentor in that hospital awakened me: "We alcoholics, when we egocentrically think the world is our oyster, soon come to realise that we have always been square pegs trying to fit into round holes. We don't fit the ways of the world, and once we allow our inner spirit to guide us, we learn to accept our lot in life as sober, humble human beings of action for others rather than ourselves. We are devoted to prayer and meditation, improving our conscious contact with God as we understand Him, praying only for knowledge of His will for us and the power to carry that out."

Some meditation methods temporarily relieved my practice, as I tried various visualisations, chanting, and mantras, seeking the most effective way to do it. Over time, I've found that deep breathing and listening to the sound of breathing in and breathing out is the most effective method for me. It brings me to stillness, slows my heart rate, and keeps me in the present moment instead of drifting off into fantasy. I learn to observe, listen, and learn. It's the nearest thing to sleep and brings peace of mind.

Sometimes, simply concentrating on prayer or reciting a rosary on beads is the most beneficial approach. Prayer seems to bring one into conscious contact with God. Focusing on the Serenity Prayer brings calmness, acceptance, mindfulness, knowledge of our spiritual condition, and, to a degree, enlightenment to our sobriety.

Sometimes, I fall into the trap of forgetting to meditate and pray. Then I lack the nourishment for the soul, the light of God's reality. The nourishment of His strength and the atmosphere of grace are supernatural gifts given to us for our salvation. To a great extent, the AA way of life upholds this truth. There is a direct link to self-examination, meditation, and prayer. These practices bring much relief and benefit when taken separately. But when they are logically related and interwoven, the result is an unshakeable foundation for life- a glimpse into the reality of the kingdom of God on earth. An assurance that He is present in all things, and we are destined to do His will if we surrender to the mystery of the plan He has for us. We are searching for a new vision, action, and grace to bear upon the opposing side of our nature in favour of the positive. It's a further step into the humility that allows God to help us. Yet, it is just one step into what He wants: we must go further.

Much has been written over time about the benefits of meditation and prayer. One of the most inspired individuals who came to terms with this is Francis of Assisi, a mystic and poet who captured the essence of prayer and meditation in his prayer:

"Lord, make me a channel (instrument) of thy peace- that where there is hatred, let me sow love - that where there is wrong, I may bring the spirit of forgiveness- that where there is discord, I may bring harmony- that where there is an error, I may bring truth- that where there is despair, I may bring hope- that where there are shadows, I may bring light- that where there is sadness, I may bring joy. Lord, grant that I may not so much seek to be consoled as to console, to be comforted as to bring comfort, to understand as to understand- to love. For it is by giving that we receive, by conformity that we are comforted, and by dying of self, we are reborn into Eternal Lift. Amen."

By rereading that prayer slowly and considering each word and sentence as guidance on how to live, we become open to the profound strength, power, beauty, and love that this prayer embodies. Here was a man who wanted to become a channel for God, asking for the grace to bring love, forgiveness, harmony, truth, hope, light, and joy to others. Then came the aspirations for himself; it is better to live in comfort than to receive it, to understand others rather than to be understood, and to forgive rather than to be forgiven. It is a perfect prayer to meditate upon the plan for salvation.

It is often said, "God genuinely works in strange ways." I was lifted from my depressed state, for I had fallen into the dragon's mouth of fear and desperation. What emerged was a lotus flower of creative ideas. The outcome of my body of work satisfied my spirit for a time, but I soon felt the trap of once more seeking ego recognition, and when I achieved it, like in former times, it was empty and unrewarding. I had another fifteen minutes of fame, but the applause soon disappeared. The lesson learnt is that I still write and create songs, but the need for egocentric applause has faded for me. I write and record more these days for the benefit of others. I have learned a great lesson, but it took a decade. Prayer and meditation are what I need, and I do not do enough of them in my life. In Paul's writings to the Thessalonians 5:16-18, he stated :

16 Rejoice always, 17 pray without ceasing, 18 give thanks in all circumstances; for this is the will of God in Christ Jesus for you.

If you wonder where Christians derive the idea that we should pray without ceasing, this is it! Paul urged the Thessalonians to make prayer a way of life. Additionally, this is easy if you're seeking a memory verse about prayer. You probably already have it memorised!

But you also need to put it into practice. As we said, this doesn't mean you must keep your head bowed, hands folded, and eyes closed all day. Instead, think of prayer as an open-ended conversation with God. You can jump back into the dialogue at any point in the day. In that sense, prayers have no end. In Luke 18, Jesus told His disciples about a widow who needed a selfish, uncaring judge to act on her behalf. Initially, he resisted her pleas. However, thanks to her persistence, he finally responded to her petition. The point is that perseverance pays off in life, especially when you persevere in prayer.

According to Paul (a very reliable source!), there is never a wrong time to pray. Every occasion, good, bad, or ordinary, calls our hearts toward our heavenly Father. While letting our minds wander is easy, we must "stay alert" and remain focused on who He is and what we are doing. Psalm 86:3: " *Be merciful to me, O Lord, for I am calling on you constantly.* "

The anonymous writer of Hebrews stated that children of the King can confidently approach His throne (Hebrews 4:16). We can be assured that we will be heard by the One who knows and loves us best. We must never forget that it's also more than that: a connection to the very One who breathed life into us. If we want to know who God is and the secrets to life that only He has, we must learn to pray without ceasing.

We must not forget that meditation and prayer are a sense of belonging that comes to us. We are constantly reminded as alcoholics that we live in the world but are no longer of the world in its materialistic way, but in a spiritual way. We are no longer frightened and sailing without a rudder. We have a purpose: It helps other alcoholics maintain sobriety. Through meditation and prayer, we glimpse the God of truth, justice, love, and the reality of eternal life. We know that God lovingly watches over us. When we turn to him, all will be well for us now and hereafter. Surprisingly, I didn't meditate and pray more constantly when writing these words. So the lesson goes on for me; writing this book is as much for me as it is for you, in living by the Steps of AA.

In my early sobriety, I encountered too much adventure in my quest for the truth of my inner purpose in life. God certainly acts in mysterious ways. First, I had to be brought down from my egocentric belief in success, my need for applause, and my measuring progress on life's path based on power, money, and prestige. Looking back, it was such a blind way of living. I experienced fifteen minutes of fame more than once in my past life, and ultimately, I found it to be an empty prize.

After a prolonged meditation, I arrived at the Steps of AA and embarked on a three-part pilgrimage to Santiago, the Way of St. James, the apostle of Christ. I came to terms with the power of the Almighty as a lotus flower of creative ideas was cast upon me. Upon returning to Australia, I began writing songs and recording them with the help of professional musicians I had come to know. Then, the urge to write books led to initial success internationally with stories related to my Camino experiences.

Thus began a quest that has lasted for over a decade. However, I fell for the trap again of the materialistic side of my nature; ego recognition was fulfilled, and money followed for a time. It was like God wanted me to see through my creative efforts that if I returned to the world and not him, I would fall again into depression. Then, returning to drinking on my third Camino pulled me up fast to the error of my ways. So, since 2017, fame and fortune have no longer been what I have been about. Instead, God has granted me the power to use my creative talents to serve him for the benefit of others and, in particular, in the services of fellow alcoholics like my former self.

"His childish sensitivity magnifies this very real feeling of inferiority, and it is this state of affairs that generates in him an insatiable, abnormal craving for self-approval and success in the eyes of the world. Still a child, he cries for the moon. And the moon, it seems, won't have him!" Language of the Heart p.102

When I entered A.A., I encountered men and women who had experienced my struggles. However, they now focus more on helping others than on themselves. They exhibited a level of selflessness I had never known. By attending meetings and engaging with them,

I considered others more and myself less. I also discovered I didn't have to rely solely on myself to escape my troubles. I could access a greater strength than my own. Am I now relying less on myself and more on God?

The next step in the program is the final one, which is the spiritual path to our happy destiny.

Many believe that beauty is defined by external factors such as clothing, makeup, hairstyles, or expensive jewellery. It is easy to become preoccupied with material possessions. However, reality is not about what we wear but who we are. The beauty that God created comes from within. It's in the twinkle of an eye that conveys a greeting, the hug that expresses love, the gentle embrace and smile that signify forgiveness, and the tear that communicates understanding. When God declared to the world, "It is good, " beauty was born. Drugs of choice and tumultuous relationships only hinder us from being what we were meant to be: beautiful for God.

Today, I strive to embody God's beauty in my actions, words, and attitudes. Father Leo's Daily Meditation

Father Leo's Daily Meditation for alcoholics is not a single, universally prescribed meditation. It refers to a collection of daily meditations written by Father Leo Booth, specifically for individuals in recovery from alcoholism and addiction. It is available in his book "Say Yes to Your Life: Daily Meditations." These meditations focus on spirituality, hope, and positive thinking, drawing inspiration from diverse sources to guide individuals in recovery. He distinguishes between the two, focusing on finding a personal connection with a higher power and finding God in everyday experiences.

CHAPTER 11.

CARRYING THE MESSAGE

So, in my recovery, I am reminded once more of Bill Wilson's life and how he came to believe in a Higher power to remain sober. Bill Wilson, or Bill W, as he was affectionately called in AA.

William Griffith "Bill" Wilson, co-founder of Alcoholics Anonymous (AA), was a stockbroker who struggled with alcoholism. Ultimately, he found recovery and dedicated his life to helping others through the fellowship he established with Dr. Bob Smith. Bill recounts how a visit from his old friend Ebby Thatcher marked the beginning of his search for a God of his understanding, a source of faith to help cure his alcoholism. Ebby had joined The Moral Rearmament (MRA), which was loosely based on the Steps of The Oxford Group. This group was founded in England in 1919 by Frank Buchman, a Lutheran minister in Oxford. The six steps of the programme served as the foundation for what followed in AA's first six steps.

Doctor Carl Jung had his view on the Oxford Group program and how it works in terms of recovery from illness:

"My attitude to these matters is that, as long as a patient is a church member, he ought to be serious. He ought to be a frank member of that church, and he should not seek to resolve his conflicts when he believes that he should do so with God. For instance, when a member of the Oxford Group comes to me to get treatment, I say: " You are in the Oxford Group, so long as you are there, you settle your affairs with the Oxford Group. I can't do better than Jesus." Collected Works vol 18, 1940.

Bill did much research into alcoholics when he became sober. He had an enlightening experience that pulled him up from the alcoholic pattern of life, and he had found through his friend Ebby a programme aligned with the Steps of the Oxford Group, but his troubles were not over.

Bill W integrated his life when at the turning point of his alcoholism whilst writing the Big Book for Alcoholics; he stated: [We were having trouble with personal relationships, we couldn't control our emotional natures, we were prey to misery and depression, we couldn't make a living, we had a feeling of uselessness, we were full of fear, we were unhappy, we couldn't seem to be of real help to other people. . . .] Alcoholics Anonymous, pg.52

These words remind me that I have more problems than alcohol, that alcohol is only a symptom of a more pervasive disease. When I stopped drinking, I began a lifetime process of recovery from unruly emotions, painful relationships, and unmanageable situations. This process is too much for most of us without help from a Higher Power and the support of our friends in the Fellowship.

When I began working the Steps of the A.A. program, many of these tangled threads unravelled, but little by little, the most broken places of my life straightened out. One day at a time, almost imperceptibly, I healed. Like a thermostat being turned down, my fears diminished. I began to experience moments of contentment. My emotions became less volatile. I am now once again a part of the human family.]

When Ebby returned to drinking after a period of sobriety, it created a sense of hopelessness for Bill W. Yet he didn't drink. He went back to his former career as a stockbroker. Wilson was in Akron for an unsuccessful business endeavour and feared relapsing. Recognising the danger, he inquired about any local alcoholics he could speak with and was referred to Smith by Henrietta Seiberling, one of the leaders of the Akron Oxford Group. Bill knew he had to share his experience to maintain his sobriety. He sought out alcoholics at Towns Hospital and Calvary Mission, attempting to spread the message of hope. Bill had been sober for five months when he met Dr. Bob on May 12, 1935.

Bill W convinced Dr. Bob that he was there not only for himself but also for Bob; he maintained that they both could achieve sobriety by helping others stay sober. Bill W's idea was to share their experiences, strength, and hope with each other and with other alcoholics. Wilson's story and ideas had an immediate impact on the doctor. In Wilson, Dr. Smith found a fellow sufferer, just like himself, who had somehow attained sobriety. Wilson explained that alcoholism was a mental, physical, and spiritual malady, an idea he had learned from Dr. William D. Silkworth of Towns Hospital in New York, where he had been a patient. Despite being a physician, Smith had never regarded alcoholism as a disease. Soon after meeting Wilson, Dr. Smith became sober and never drank again.

Dr Bob died on 16th November 1950, having helped over 5000 alcoholics maintain sobriety over the remaining 15 years of his life. Bill Wilson maintained sobriety for the final thirty-six years of his life. He went on to write many books on spirituality, belief in a higher power, sobriety and the most renowned Big Book of AA. Bill had looked at many alternative cures for alcoholism over a lifetime. Bill W used LSD in the 1950s when he recalled his spiritual awakening at Towns Hospital in December 1934.

In a letter to Doctor Carl Jung in March 1961, Bill wrote, "On my first trial several years ago, my original spontaneous spiritual experience of twenty-five years before was re-enacted in wonderful splendour and conviction" (Wilson, letter to Jung, March 1961). Bill tried many cures for his alcoholism, as he was often depressed during the decades following his sobriety. He discovered the benefits of taking large quantities of Vitamin B to help alleviate his depression. When asked about his most outstanding achievement, he replied, " Discovering the health benefits of Vitamin B."

While Bill went on to write many books on spirituality, physical health, and alcoholism, we alcoholics recognise the Big Book, first published in 1939, as his most outstanding achievement, not to mention all those he helped through AA sponsorship. Bill Wilson maintained his sobriety from alcohol until his death. He was also a heavy cigarette smoker, and at age 75, on June 24, 1971, he died.

One of the most essential ideas emerging from this is simple and frequently repeated in AA meetings worldwide: "Don't take the first drink, and you can't get drunk!" AA introduced the concept that a physical allergy combined with a mental obsession leads to an inability to stop drinking. Thanks to Bill and many others, the notion that individuals can form their understanding of a Higher Power has enabled many sceptics to achieve sobriety through the Twelve Steps.

Bill W.'s introductory textbook of Alcoholics Anonymous, published in 1939, explains AA's principles, the core of which is the now well-known Twelve Steps. Alcoholics Anonymous is now a worldwide organisation with groups in virtually every country on the planet and a membership in the millions. It is widely acknowledged as the most successful recovery program in existence.

The old saying, " actions speak louder than words, " is indeed true, especially for alcoholics striving to remain sober. It seems that the twelfth step- " Having had a spiritual awakening as a result of these steps, we tried to carry this message to alcoholics and to practice these principles in all our affairs"- is key to living a new way of life, staying free from drink one day at a time, and gaining the gift of the spirit when we help another suffering alcoholic do the same.

Here, we express a giving that carries no material reward. We begin to practise the Steps in our daily lives. Step 12 emphasises helping fellow individuals struggling with alcohol addiction to achieve sobriety, fostering a sense of community and maintaining spiritual growth—this effort to prioritise others before ourselves is humbling in its way.

The first and foremost Spiritual Principle in Step Twelve is service. The Twelfth Step would be a culmination of all the previous steps. In a way, it is, but we have also been introduced to a few new ones. Among them is Service, which serves as the basis for this Step; we are grateful for that. Many people find the 12th Step of Alcoholics Anonymous to be one of the most challenging because it forces them to publicly acknowledge their struggles with alcohol when delivering the AA message to others.

After completing the 12th Step, some people feel a sense of relief, as though they have graduated from the AA program. Although it is important to feel proud of your accomplishments, it is just as important to remember that recovery is a lifelong journey, and your participation in Alcoholics Anonymous isn't over. However, for some people, the sense of completing the AA program brings back their urge to drink.

Some people feel that by completing Alcoholics Anonymous Step 12, they have proven that they are capable of living a sober life and can drink alcohol in moderation. For alcoholics, this is a false premise. We can never forget that the first drink does all the damage: "One is too many, and a thousand is not enough," as the saying goes. Remember, we are alcoholics and can only remain firm against the desire to drink by seeking the support of a sponsor, the AA community by continuing to attend meetings, and, as our founders proved time and again, helping some others still suffering from alcohol while maintaining sobriety. And not the least of these is surrendering to a Higher Power.

To "surrender," whether in prayer, thought, or deed, is to yield our will to a higher purpose, relinquishing control over the outcomes we try to dictate. This age-old practice, deeply rooted in Scripture, carries a common thread of peace and release. Surrender aligns us with the essence of our relationship with God, acknowledging His power and humble submission to His will. Here are eight acts of surrender that will allow you to put God first every day.

The message of surrender is as much a reminder to myself as to you, the reader:

By dedicating the first moments of our day to meditation and prayer, we offer the day itself to God's guidance. In these peaceful moments, verses like Psalms 143:8 can soothe our souls: "Let the morning bring me word of your unfailing love, for I have put my trust in you."

The words of Proverbs 3:5-6 tell us, "Trust in the Lord with all your heart; do not depend on your understanding. Seek his will in all you do, and he will show you which path to take."

Through these words, our lives intertwine with His divine story. A grateful heart sets the stage for surrender. Every day presents numerous opportunities to be thankful, whether for the beauty of life itself or the small blessings we encounter each day.

As with the Big Book of AA, the Twelve Steps and Twelve Traditions, daily reflection readings, and indeed the Scriptures, engaging with the God of one's understanding allows for a dialogue between our hearts and God. In the Biblical Psalm 119
The Psalmist declares, "Your word is a lamp for my feet, a light on my path." With His truth shining on our path, surrendering becomes more apparent, and we can confidently walk forward. Then, we must find time for silence, too. Intentional silence positions us to hear the gentle whisper of the Holy Spirit.

In our 12-step work, serving others becomes an offering of love—a love that mirrors Jesus' example. As Mark 10:45 reminds us, "For even the Son of Man came not to be served but to serve others and to give his life as a ransom for many." In each selfless act, we surrender our comforts for the sake of others, putting God's priorities into practice.

We must also not forget that we are forgiven for our defective nature and must strive to understand the depth of God's forgiveness. Through forgiveness, we rid ourselves of bitterness and align our hearts with God's. The Lord's Prayer in Matthew 6:14-15 emphasises this: "For if you forgive others their trespasses, your heavenly Father will also forgive you, but if you do not forgive others their trespasses, neither will your Father forgive your trespasses."

It's a good time to reflect before we go to sleep. Remember to review the day's activities, not only by handing them over to God but also by praying for the ancestral spirits of our past. It is written: "It's a Holy and wholesome thought to pray for the dead so they may be freed from their sins." Our introspection can become a conversation with God, a soul-searching that strengthens our commitment and sets the stage for tomorrow's surrender.

We should set aside time for daily surrender through prayer and meditation, renewing our constant connection with God, the spirit that dwells within us, if we believe it is so. Its acceptance helps our journey with Jesus of the Spirit.

CHAPTER 12.

THE ANCESTRY OF JESUS

Some readers may stop at this book's biblical accounts of Jesus' lineage. That's acceptable if you have enough information to incorporate the Steps of AA into your life or if you've grasped, to some extent, the significance of the book's title, which pertains to spiritual action with Christ as your Higher Power. However, I feel compelled to explore Jesus' ancestral line further, as it connects to being filled with His Spirit and His ultimate sacrifice, so that we may be saved.

The Book of Genesis, translated as "origin" from Greek, sets the stage for the Bible's redemptive narrative. The story begins with God confronting chaos and disorder to establish order and beauty within creation. Humans are formed and appointed to engage in God's divine rule over the universe.

It demonstrated how God created the world and engaged with all humanity until He established a personal relationship with Abraham, their forefather. Genesis unveiled God's eternal promises to Abraham, Isaac, and Jacob—promises that extended to their descendants. Most readers of Genesis and many scholars focus on the covenant in Genesis 15, which concerns Abraham as the father of the nation of Israel; however, they also consider the covenant in Genesis 17.

We learn about our creation, the origins of sin and its consequences, and how to relate to God best through obedience and trust. We are immersed in stories of deceit, jealousy, and outright failure, where we see how God continues to work through flawed individuals.

According to the biblical book of Genesis, Abraham departed from Ur in Mesopotamia after God called him to establish a new nation in a yet-to-be-specified land, which he would later discover was the land of Canaan. He followed God's commands, to whom he received repeated promises and a covenant that his "seed" would inherit the land.

In an earthly sense, Jesus connects with Abraham's descendants through His lineage, as He is a descendant of Abraham and King David. He assists by offering forgiveness of sins and establishing a new covenant for all people. First, referring to Jesus as the Son of David underscores His dual nature: He is truly human and divine. Second, this title indicates that Jesus is Israel's promised Messiah who will inherit the throne of His ancestor, David.

What does it signify that Jesus is called the Son of David? Matthew begins His genealogy by identifying Jesus as "the son of David, the son of Abraham" (Matt. 1:1). This title is rooted in God's promise to David in 2 Samuel 7:12-16, where God promises to establish the kingdom of one of David's descendants.

The Lord promised that the Dravidic throne would be established "forever" (v. 16), and the prophets echoed this promise. Isaiah 11:10 describes the Messiah's reign and refers to Him as "the Root of Jesse" (see Rev. 5:5; 22:16). Jesse was David's father. Jeremiah and Zechariah reference this by calling the Messiah a "Branch" (Jer. 23:5; 33:15; Zech. 3:8; 6:12).

Jesus did not object to being called the Son of David (Matt. 9:27; 12:23; 21:15, 16). Matthew and Mark link Jesus to David in their genealogies (Matt. 1:1, 6, 17; Luke 3:31). Three implications of the title are outlined in Luke 1:32-33. First, referring to Jesus as the Son of David emphasises the two natures of Christ: He is both truly human and truly divine. Second, this title indicates that Jesus is Israel's promised Messiah who will inherit the throne of His ancestor, David. Third, Jesus will rule over a kingdom that will never come to an end.

Because He was Israel's Messiah and the Son of David, Jesus was sent first to Israel. This understanding helps us better comprehend why Jesus declined the Canaanite woman's plea for help. "I was sent only to the lost sheep of Israel," Jesus told her (Matt. 15:24). However, when she pointed out that even the dogs eat crumbs that fall from their master's table, Jesus praised her faith and granted her request (v. 28). Jesus' initial refusal did not mean He was uninterested in Gentiles. Including Gentiles in the promises made to David has always been part of God's plan (Acts 15:12-18).

Jesus' human lineage made Him a descendant of David. However, we must not forget that His divine nature renders Him more significant than David. In one of His final confrontations with the Pharisees, Jesus stated that the Son of David was also David's Lord (Matt. 22:41-46; Ps. 110:1). As the Son of David, Jesus is our Saviour, King, and Lord.

In the Bible, the book of Exodus tells the story of the Israelites' enslavement, the Plagues of Egypt, their departure from Egypt, the revelations at Mount Sinai, and their wanderings in the wilderness up to the borders of Canaan.   Exodus recounts Israel's liberation from oppression in Egypt, the formation of God's covenant with Israel, the reception of essential commandments at Sinai, Israel's paradigmatic rebellion during the Golden Calf incident, and the faithful construction of the Tabernacle.

The theme of Exodus is **redemption—how God delivered the Israelites and made them His special people.** After rescuing them from slavery, God provided the Law, which offered instructions on how the people could be consecrated or made holy.

Exodus illustrates how **God prevented Pharaoh from further oppressing and destroying the Israelites.** The book also reveals how God led the people of Israel into the wilderness to cultivate them into one people. He intended them to be. Exodus serves as a reminder that after deliverance comes development.

During their travels in the wilderness, the people of Israel were commanded to build a tabernacle so that God could "dwell among them" (Exodus 29:46). The term "tabernacle " means 'place of dwelling' and was named under the belief that God lived within its sacred confines. In short, the Tabernacle was a tent where Israel could meet God during their journeys in the wilderness. In other words, the Tabernacle functioned as a *mobile temple*. After entering the promised land, Israel would eventually construct a permanent temple under King Solomon's reign. When Solomon dedicated the temple, the priests brought the Tabernacle and the Ark of the Covenant to Jerusalem: " And they brought up the ark of the Lord, the tent of meeting, and all the holy vessels in the tent; the priests and the Levites brought them up. " (1 Kg 8:4) ESV)

Thomas Aquinas identified the uniqueness of Scripture in its ability not only for its words to represent an object in the world (this is normal) but also for these objects to point beyond themselves to some other reality. The reason why created objects carry meaning beyond themselves is that God created them to do so. For example, the heavens above declare the glory of God (Psalm 19:1). Therefore, the sky has meaning because God imbued it with meaning when He created it; this meaning is objective, not subjective. Likewise, God gave the Tabernacle significance. It refers to a mobile temple in Israel's time and points to Christ and the New Covenant.

Ruth, a Moabite woman, appears in the Book of Ruth in the Old Testament and holds significance for Jesus, as she is included in His genealogy in the Gospel of Matthew. She is the great-grandmother of King David, from whom Jesus is also descended. Through her faith, Ruth becomes a significant figure in Israel's history. Because of the Lord's faithfulness to Ruth and Boaz, the world received the Messiah, who shows equal respect to those the wider community despised and regarded as outsiders.

The global message of Ruth applies wherever ethnic strife occurs—whether in the discriminatory treatment of the Dalit people in India, the brutal genocides in countries like Rwanda and Sudan, the atrocities in Croatia, Serbia, and Bosnia, or the sporadic antagonism towards immigrants in North America.

The gospel of Jesus Christ is the only cure for ethnic strife, but its teaching that all are equal, accepted, and loved in Christ must penetrate the depths of the heart and soul of the global church. The book of Ruth demonstrates that the Lord delights in accepting ethnic outsiders into His community, provided they come through faith in Christ. The faithful town of Bethlehem also understood this was the way of the Lord when its community embraced Ruth (Ruth 4:11-12, 14-15; compare Gen. 28; Col 3:11).

First, Samuel is set in the land of Israel, where the Hebrews invaded and settled (see Joshua). Numerous other people continued to dwell alongside Israel, often disrupting the peace and encouraging the Israelites to stray from their faith.

In this critical period of Israel's history, the people of God transformed from a loosely affiliated group of tribes into a unified nation under a form of government headed by a king. They traded the turmoil of life under the judges for the stability of a strong central monarchy.

First, Samuel focuses on establishing the monarchy. The people demanded a king, similar to the kings of the surrounding nations (1 Samuel 8:5). Saul, the first king, though "head and shoulders above the rest," did not have a righteous heart. His line was destined never to inherit the crown (9:1 15:35). God instructed Samuel to anoint David, the youngest son of Jesse of Bethlehem, as the next king (16:1 13).

Much of 1 Samuel follows David's exploits as a young musician, shepherd, and warrior. We witness his underdog victory over Goliath (17:1-58), his deep friendship with Jonathan (18:1-4), and his growing military prowess (18:5-30). He waited patiently for the throne, often pursued and driven into hiding by Saul.

First, Samuel chronicles the beginning of Israel's monarchy, following the lives of the prophet Samuel, the ill-fated King Saul, and God's ultimate choice of David as king. Several themes feature prominently.

Providence: God repeatedly made everyday events serve His purposes. He used Hannah's contentious relationship with Peninnah, a

Hebrew woman in 1 Samuel 1:1-28, to lead Saul to Samuel during Saul's search for lost donkeys (9:1-27). He caused David to learn of Goliath while bringing food to his brothers (17:1-58). These are just a few examples.

Kingship: As the divine King, God designated a human vice-regent, David, to rule over His people. This history validates David's house as the legitimate ruler of Israel. It also fulfils Jacob's promise that the sceptre will never depart Judah, David's tribe (Genesis 49:10).

Reversal of human fortune: Hannah's barrenness gave way to children (1 Samuel 1:1–28; 2:21); Samuel became prophet instead of Eli's sons (2:12; 3:13); Saul rose to prominence though he was from a lowly tribe; and David was anointed king though he was the youngest son (16:1–13). God reversed standard human patterns so His plan could be furthered, showing His sovereignty over all.

God is still sovereign in the twenty-first century. He will accomplish His purposes with or without our cooperation. However, as confirmed in the lives of Samuel, Saul, and David, our response to God's call has a significant impact on our outcome. Will we obey Him as Samuel and David did and live lives marked by blessing? Or will we, like Saul, try to live on our terms? "To obey is better than sacrifice," Samuel told Saul (1 Samuel 15:22). That truth still speaks to us today.

The 1 and 2 books of Kings record Israel's prolonged struggle between true and false worship. From the reign of King Solomon until his exile to Babylon—nearly 400 years—the prophets of God clashed with the kings of Israel and Judah regarding their idolatrous behaviour. Since God's predictions about exile are eventually fulfilled, the prophets have the last word over those kings who follow other gods. In this way, the Lord shows himself superior to all other spiritual powers, including the false gods that many of Israel's faithless kings follow.

Amid the chorus of idols beckoning for the attention of God's people both in ancient times and today, only the God and Father of our Lord Jesus Christ reign supreme and deserves our trust.

In 1 Kings, the Lord's sovereignty over other powers is most powerfully expressed in the confrontation between the prophet Elijah and the prophets of Baal on Mount Carmel (1 Kings 18). This story is often cited as an example of a "power encounter"—a method for triumphing over the forces of darkness. Advocates of such approaches to spiritual warfare typically argue that power encounters are essential for achieving breakthroughs for the gospel, particularly in animistic and tribal contexts. However, the broader context of 1 Kings 17-18 suggests that "truth encounters" and "power encounters" often work in tandem to demonstrate that the Lord is superior to all false gods.

[Like the books of Samuel and Kings, 1 and 2 Chronicles were also written as a single book in the Hebrew Bible. However, many modern readers skip over it when it repeats much of the material from the previous books. Chronicles is the final book in the Hebrew Bible, summarising the ongoing relationship between God and Israel through Abraham's blessing. The structure of Chronicles encourages readers to explore the stories within each section, revealing intriguing details about David, Solomon, God's temple, the kings of Judah, and how they all interconnect. Chronicles also serve as an excellent historical reference for those studying specific facts and Scriptures.] Google search.

Nehemiah was a Hebrew living in Persia, where he served the king. After hearing a bad report from one of his brothers, he wanted to go to Jerusalem and rebuild the temple of God. God was pleased that Nehemiah was committed to serving him and made it possible for him to return. God blessed Nehemiah's work.

The Book of Esther recounts the story celebrated during Purim, in which Queen Esther and her cousin Mordecai rescue the Jewish people from Haman's wicked plot. Haman, an advisor to the Persian King Ahasuerus, attempted to annihilate the Jews.

In the Book of Job, a pious man is tested by God to show that his faith is not tied to his material possessions. However, Job begins to question why he has lost everything, but eventually admits that he does not have God's wisdom and cannot know everything.

The Book of Psalms, a collection of 150 Hebrew poems, songs, and prayers, serves as a prayer book for God's people. It focuses on praise, lament, faith, and hope, reflecting Israel's history and the anticipation of the Messiah.

The chief concern of Proverbs is the pursuit of a happy and good life on earth, lived in the context of a faithful calling. The Book of Proverbs also has a speculative aspect about the world's order that invites folks to live in the ways various proverbs suggest.

The book of Ecclesiastes is the author's response to the book of Proverbs. From their perspective, life isn't so simple as fearing God and choosing wisdom. Life is fleeting and unpredictable; our existence is a blip of time. In their words, "It's all meaningless." So, is there any point at all? The Ecclesiastic's wisdom probably comes from Solomon. It summarises the meaning of life as living according to God's will, where all one can expect from life as a reward is to enjoy good food and drink in the company of friends, offering it all to God.

The sovereign Lord is watching—a saving God. But warning gives way to merciful promises of salvation. The message of the Book of Isaiah to the world is that there is indeed a Saviour, the Messiah, who has humbly, painfully, and gloriously won salvation for sinners and all who trust in him.

The book of Jeremiah begins with God calling Jeremiah to be a prophet and giving him a dual vocation. He was to be a prophet to Israel and the nations, and his words would "uproot and tear down" and also "plant and build up" (er.1:10). In other words, Jeremiah was to accuse Israel and warn them of God's coming judgment, but he was also to give a message of hope for the future. This introduction perfectly summarises the first large section, chapters 1-24, consisting of a collection of Jeremiah's writings before the exile.

The Book of Lamentations is a tribute to the pain and confusion the Israelites experienced after the destruction of their Temple. This memorial illustrates the importance of prayerful lament in our faith journey through a broken world.

The Book of Ezekiel is the third of the Latter Prophets in the Hebrew Bible and one of the major prophetic books in the Christian Bible, following Isiah and Jeremiah. The book records six visions of the prophet Ezekiel, exiled in Babylon, during the 22 years from 593 to 571 BC. It is the product of a long and complex history and does not necessarily preserve the prophets. The visions and the book are structured around three themes: (1) judgment on Israel (chapters 1–24), (2) judgment on the nations (chapters 25–32), and (3) future blessings for Israel (chapters 33–48).[3] Its themes include the concepts of God's presence, purity, Israel as a divine community, and individual responsibility to God. Its later influence has included the development of mystical and apocalyptic traditions in Second Temple Judaism, Rabbinic Judaism, and Christianity.

The message of the Book of Daniel is that, just as the God of Israel saved Daniel and his friends from their enemies, he would save all of Israel from their present oppression. This book tells of their struggles to maintain hope in the land of their conquerors. Daniel's experiences provide hope and assurance that God will confront evil and deliver his people.

The Book of Hosea is about God's loving relationship with the chosen people — a love that leads God to judge them when they love others and oppress one another. While God should and sometimes does bring justice to human evil, his purpose and heart are ultimately to heal and save. And that is Hosea's message to all future generations.

The Book of Joel is a Jewish prophetic text containing a series of "divine announcements". The first line attributes authorship to "Joel the son of Pethuel. "Joel spends most of his time writing about the Day of the Lord. The Day of the Lord is a prevalent theme throughout the Minor Prophets, serving as a declaration of God's judgment on evil, both past and future. This judgment is for the nation of Judah, Jerusalem, and the people of God, Israel.

The Book of Amos is the third of the Twelve Minor Prophets in the Old Testament and the second in the Greek Septuagint tradition. The Book of Amos has nine chapters. Amos had a passion for justice. He was a prophet "par excellence" of social justice. The message of the book of Amos can be presented under three basic themes or theological motifs defined by justice, namely: (1) justice among the nations, (2) justice in the nation, and (3) justice and piety of a nation.

The theme of Jonah is God's saving mercy toward the nations of the world. The Lord's compassion is not only for insiders like Jonah and Israel but also for outsiders like the Ninevites. Jonah vividly displays God's heart of mercy for all people groups of the world, even those known for their godlessness.

Three of the Bible's great themes form the backbone of Micah: divine judgment of sin, merciful restoration due to God's covenant faithfulness, achieved through a coming Shepherd-King, and the compassion that God's people must accordingly demonstrate to a watching world.

Nahum is one of the minor prophets in the Old Testament, classified as a prophet of God. He is mentioned only once in the entire book of Nahum. He receives a vision about the city of Nineveh, its destruction due to evil practices, and its turning away from the Lord again after being given a chance previously.

Confidence in the Lord is the key theme of Habakkuk. It is. It is a universal need for God's people worldwide and throughout history. God can and must be trusted at all costs, as Christ has proven to us supremely.

Zephaniah's central theme is the day of the Lord. It elucidates two significant aspects of this theme: judgment and restoration. In both aspects, Zephaniah evinces many parallels to the books of the eighth-century prophets.

Haggai reminds us of our challenges today and to remain faithful to God's covenant. Haggai challenges the returned exiles to stay loyal and rebuild the temple. The recently returned exiles face hardship in their rebuilding efforts and struggle to remain faithful after much loss and disappointment. Haggai assures the people that their efforts and faithfulness will be blessed.

The Book of Zechariah contains descriptions of visions concerning the rebuilding of Jerusalem and the temple, the gathering of scattered Israel, and Israel's triumph over its enemies. The book culminates in prophecies of the Saviour's mortal ministry and final return in glory.

Malachi's oracles indict the human condition and Israel's selfishness and sin. This book reiterates God's promise that He will one day send a messenger to confront evil, restore His people, and bring healing justice.

In summary, in the Old Testament, God tells Abraham to sacrifice his son, Isaac, on Mount Moriah. Abraham prepares to obey God's command, despite loving Isaac dearly. At the last moment, God intervenes, providing a ram as a substitute sacrifice, thereby saving Isaac's life.

Christians interpret this story as a prefiguration of Jesus's sacrifice on the cross. Isaac, the beloved son of Abraham, is seen as a type of Jesus, the beloved Son of God. The ram sacrificed in Isaac's place is viewed as foreshadowing Jesus, the "Lamb of God" who takes away the world's sins. Just as God provided a ram for Abraham, He provided Jesus as the ultimate sacrifice for humanity's sins. God's covenant with Abraham, which promises him a great nation and the blessing of all people through him, is also interpreted as leading to Jesus, who fulfils that promise.
Jesus, a descendant of Abraham, is the one through whom God's promise is fulfilled. Through Jesus, individuals from all nations

can receive spiritual blessings and salvation, fulfilling God's covenant.

The entire Bible points to Jesus, and this is especially true of the book of Genesis. This passage is like a lock, and Jesus is the key. Consider the parallels between this story and Jesus' story.

Both Isaac and Jesus are long-awaited "beloved sons" born under miraculous circumstances (Gen. 22:1; Matt. 3:17). Each son carries the wood that will serve as the instrument of their deaths on their backs (Gen. 22:6; John 19:17). In both narratives, the father leads the son up a mountain, while the son follows obediently toward his death (Gen. 22:3; Matt. 26:39). Furthermore, in both scenarios, God provides the sacrificial substitute, which Abraham specifies will be a ram (a male lamb), as noted by the New Testament authors in Genesis 22:8 and John 1:29.

Abraham and Isaac point beyond themselves to the Messiah. This story is a prophetic reenactment of the greater redemption God would someday accomplish through one of their descendants, Jesus.

St. Thomas Aquinas, a great religious scholar and theologian, held that Sacred Scripture, divinely ordered, reveals truths necessary for salvation and that the literal sense of Scripture is fundamental for theological argumentation, with spiritual interpretations built upon it. Aquinas believed that Sacred Scripture exists to reveal the truth necessary for salvation, situating it within God's plan for humanity's participation in divine life.

Aquinas believed that humans are created in the image of God (imago Dei), possessing reason, intellect, and free will, which enable them to participate in the divine order and discover their true purpose through their relationships with God and others. This inherent capacity for reason and intellect signifies that humans are not merely biological beings but also spiritual beings, capable of understanding and participating in the divine order. In its intellectual nature, the human soul is seen as the locus of the image of God, making humans capable of knowing and loving God and, consequently, belonging to God.

Behind every company's symbol in modern society lies a story that encompasses its foundation, current mission statement, and logo—a blend of text and visual imagery.

In the Bible's story, symbolism plays a significant role in faith. An exchange occurs in <u>Genesis 22</u>: the ram substitutes for Isaac. This message points to the greater exchange at the cross, where the Son of God takes humanity's place. In Jesus, God delivers his promised Son through death and beyond. Just as God spared Isaac, he spared humanity by bearing the cross himself. The symbol of the Cross resonates with anyone who has embraced the Spirit of Christ through the Steps of AA as the Higher Power. Similarly, the symbolic meaning of the Trinity —the Father, the Son, and the Holy Spirit —is evident to those in the Christian faith.

The crucifix is a sign of Jesus's sacrifice for humanity. Like any icon, it reminds us of our need for repentance, self-sacrifice for others, and union with the spirit within. It is a visual image of Christ suffering and dying for humanity's salvation.

The triangle symbol in AA reflects the three principles or legacies of our program (recovery, unity, and service) that are the remedies to the three-part disease of alcoholism (physical, mental, and spiritual). The use of the circle that surrounds the triangle depicts Alcoholics Anonymous in its entirety. To the Atheist and Agnostic, the

AA insignia may well be a logical, linear sign of a different kind of trinity, which parallels the spiritual realm of those who have embraced the spirit of Jesus as their Higher Power, just as equally as the Christian principle of Father, Son, and Holy Spirit.

The triangle symbol in AA reflects the three principles or legacies of our program (recovery, unity, and service) that are the remedies to the three-part disease of alcoholism (physical, mental, and spiritual). The use of the circle that surrounds the triangle depicts Alcoholics Anonymous in its entirety. St. Thomas Aquinas has the last word in this Chapter, for he believed that there is no contradiction between revelation and reason, and that Scripture is written in metaphors that render the divine mystery meaningful for finite human minds.

CHAPTER 13.

EPILOGUE

So, summarising this book as it relates to spiritual progress, emphasising the God of your understanding, may leave you sceptical of my mission towards Jesus and taking the spirit therein on board. As you surrender to the programme and the Steps, give the Jesus spirit a try, for you may be pleasantly surprised.

We in AA may not see it as an affiliation with a religious organisation or a shared goal. Nevertheless, regardless of how one perceives it, we have a mission or a faith that helps us remain sober, at least spiritually, one day at a time, and we share a common purpose.

"True belonging occurs only when we present our authentic, imperfect selves to the world. Our sense of belonging can never exceed our level of self-acceptance." -Brené Brown.
Brene Brown is a researcher and storyteller who's spent the past two decades studying courage, vulnerability, shame, and empathy, and says: "Belonging starts with self-acceptance. Your level of belonging can never be greater than your level of self-acceptance because believing you're enough gives you the courage to be authentic, vulnerable, and imperfect."

The Bible is a means of understanding God's purpose for humankind, of belonging in the service of his divine mission. The AA Big Book teaches us the commitment to belonging to God, the AA fellowship, and our duties to others. Each of us can instantly assess whether we belong in any given situation. We can also do the same for anyone we meet. However, in the world at large, it sometimes doesn't work. Here is another reason why it is also wise to belong spiritually to a fellowship that shares your values of being in this world but not of the world. In a claim for unity, we will find that the starting point in this consideration will be our sense of belonging. The most critical step to spiritual progress is fellowship with others. Membership in AA for alcoholics is paramount in maintaining sobriety. And belief in a higher power in our lives is the key to unlocking the door to strength, unity, service, and ultimate recovery.

I encourage the reader to consult the Big Book of AA for guidance with the Steps, read Bill and Bob's stories, and explore Bible narratives that relate to Jesus and living in the spirit. Be mindful that, despite our efforts, the simplicity of Christ's guiding messages, embedded in the Bible and those within the AA Steps, reminds us that we all fail occasionally. If we don't make mistakes, we do not make progress. We are those who, despite failure, rise again with hope and faith that God will continue to set us free. We believe that God forgives us for our character defects, which is sufficient. We should not feel lost or bewildered in our understanding of our spiritual dilemma, as stated in The Big Book, "How It Works" Chapter 5. When confronted with the 12 Steps for Recovery, we may exclaim, "What an order! I can't go through with it." Do not be discouraged; none of us has consistently adhered to these principles. We are not saints. The point is that we are willing. We claim spiritual progress, not spiritual perfection.

"We found that the principles of tolerance and love must be emphasised in practice. We can never say (or insinuate) to anyone that he must agree to our formula or face excommunication. An atheist may stand up in an A.A. meeting, still denying the Deity, yet reporting how significantly he has changed in attitude and outlook.

Much experience indicates he will eventually change his mind about God, but nobody tells him he must do so.

"To further promote the principles of inclusiveness and tolerance, we impose no religious requirements on anyone. Anyone struggling with alcohol who wishes to overcome their issue and find a happy adjustment in their life can become an A.A. member simply by associating with us. Only sincerity is required. However, we do not demand even that. "

In such an atmosphere, the orthodox, the unorthodox, and the believer can mix happily and usefully. Opportunities for spiritual growth are available to all.

Tolerance in Practice, As Bill Sees It.Pg 158.

I hope you will embrace the content of this book and embody the message of its title, "Into Action: Alcoholics for Jesus," drawing valuable insights from its pages to help you stay sober one day at a time. Despite your struggles, I encourage you to grow in the likeness and image of God while sharing this message with alcoholics who are still in need.

Authors Comments.

In 1936, a new thought movement book offering readers a fresh perspective on living became an instant bestseller. It was titled "How to Win Friends and Influence People " by Dale Carnegie. This was closely followed in 1937 by another self-help book, " Think and Grow Rich" by Napoleon Hill. The radio interviews of the two authors across the nation and in the news in New York City could not have escaped the notice of Bill Wilson, co-founder of AA, who may have realised the potential of writing the Big Book of AA based on the success of those two self-help books. It is known that soon after completing the Dale Carnegie Course and reading Napoleon Hill's book, in May 1938, Bill began writing "Alcoholics Anonymous: A Story of How More than One Hundred Men Have Recovered from Alcoholism." A year later, the book was printed and ready for purchase and reading. Historical records indicate that Bill Wilson was well-read in self-help, nutrition, and spirituality. Therefore, there is no indication that he plagiarised ideas from Carnegie's or Hill's successful books, as he seems more influenced by the six-step programme of the Oxford Group and the spiritual writings of William James and Carl Jung than by any others. Both William James and Carl Jung were later recognised as founders of AA.

As to the book itself, the shared experiences of many members are included. However, the author has conceived a recommended process for maintaining sobriety. We learn from Chapters Five and Six, "How It Works " and "Into Action " (the middle of the book)- this critical juncture in the story is the most important, for nothing is more central to the book Alcoholics Anonymous than the program of recovery outlined in the Twelve Steps. Unfortunately, no primary documents mention the actual writing of the steps. These two chapters about the Steps were the last written and completed under the pressure of the eleventh hour. It appears that Bill wrote six steps using the Oxford Group template and introduced the final six as necessary complements to the others, all of which were completed two weeks before publication. A team of four editors over the twelve months before print honed the masterpiece into a saleable package.

Bill Wilson was always a complex person with multiple ambitions and influences. In his former life as a drinker, he dreamed great dreams of power, dreams of domination. He once said, "Money, to me, was never a symbol of security. It was the symbol of prestige and power." He dreamed of the day when he would sit on prestigious boards of directors. 'J.P. Morgan and First National Bank were his heroes.' Bill learnt that his lot was to take the road less travelled to help other alcoholics maintain sobriety. His was no longer the ways of the world as such, but the ways of the spirit.

We do know that co-founder Bob Smith discouraged Bill W from focusing the Big Book on its commercial value. Initially, the newly formed AA fellowship printed only 100 copies and barely broke even on printing costs.

Interestingly, the last statistics on copies of the Big Book sold in 2012 totalled 37,000,000, and it is printed in 70 different languages from its original English translation. It is considered one of the best-selling books of all time; in 2012, the Library of Congress nominated The Big Book as one of the most influential books that have shaped America.

The biblical timeline spans approximately 4,000 years, from Adam to Jesus, encompassing the Old Testament (from creation to Jesus' death) and the New Testament (which covers Jesus' life, teachings, and the early church). This timeline encompasses key events, including the creation, the Flood, the Patriarchs (Abraham, Isaac, and Jacob), the Exodus, the reign of David, the Babylonian exile, and the birth, life, death, and resurrection of Jesus. The earliest complete printed edition of the Bible was the Gutenberg Bible, produced in the 1450s by Johannes Gutenberg in Mainz, Germany. This marked the beginning of printing in Europe using mass-produced, movable metal type. The Bible has been printed and distributed in about 5 billion copies worldwide, translated into hundreds of languages, and remains the most published book in history.

While this little work, " Into Action: Alcoholics for Jesus, " draws on thoughts from the Bible and the Big Book of AA, it serves more as a reference for alcoholics to consider embracing Jesus as a Higher Power rather than merely adopting a suggested philosophy of life from either the Bible or the Big Book of AA. This theme may encourage others to expand upon it, as professional editors or scribes have not influenced me in my writing. While some may find fault with this book's directive for believers, which also includes atheists and agnostics, I see no reason to change anything herein. I'm reminded of when Pilate, the Roman Governor, inscribed on the cross above Jesus the Latin INRI, "Iesus Nazarenus Rex Iudaeorum," which translates as " Jesus of Nazareth, King of the Jews. "The High Priest wanted him to change it, but he replied, "What I've written, I've written. "This declaration continues to be used today on crosses and crucifixes.

About the Author

Doug McPhillips, poet, singer, songwriter, and author, commenced his journey of discovery over a decade ago after life-changing experiences.

The many tracks he has traversed through the Northern Hemisphere and down under in Australia and New Zealand have inspired both the facts and fiction of this novel.

Doug has written twenty-three novels and three album collections, all inspired by his adventures. Besides his creative pursuits, he devotes time to family, friends, and those who benefit most from his efforts and expertise.

TABLE OF CONTENTS

INTRODUCTION. Pg. 5.

CHAPTER 1. POWERLESS. Pg. 9.

CHAPTER 2. CAME TO BELIEVE. Pg. 19

CHAPTER 3. TURNING TO GOD. Pg. 29.

CHAPTER 4. A MORAL INVENTORY. Pg. 39.

CHAPTER 5. AN ADMISSION TO GOD. Pg. 49

CHAPTER 6. THE GIFT OF RELEASE. Pg. 59.

CHAPTER 7. HUMILITY. Pg. 69.

CHAPTER 8. MORE ON MAKING AMENDS. Pg. 79.

CHAPTER 9. AWARENESS IN SPIRIT. Pg. 89.

CHAPTER 10. SPIRITUAL GRATITUDE. Pg. 99.

CHAPTER 11. CARRYING THE MESSAGE. Pg. 107.

CHAPTER 12. THE ANCESTRY OF JESUS. Pg. 115.

CHAPTER 13. EPILOGUE. Pg.131.

29/6/25 amended copy.

www.ingramcontent.com/pod-product-compliance
Lightning Source LLC
Chambersburg PA
CBHW061209070526
44583CB00025B/3173